Shire County Guide 13

D1149038

BUCKINGHAMSHIRE

Ian F. W. Beckett

Shire Publications Ltd

Published in 1995 by Shire Publications Ltd, Cromwell House, Church Street, Princes Risborough, Buckinghamshire HP27 9AA, UK.
Copyright © 1995 by Ian F. W. Beckett. First published 1987. Enlarged second edition 1995.
Shire County Guide 13. ISBN 0 7478 0270 X.

Printed in Great Britain by CIT Printing Services, Press Buildings, Merlins Bridge, Haverfordwest, Dyfed SA61 1XF.

British Library Cataloguing in Publication Data: Beckett, I. F. W. Buckinghamshire. – 2Rev.ed. – (Shire County Guides; No.13) I. Title II. Series 914.25904. ISBN 0-7478-0270-X.

Acknowledgements

The photographs are by Cadbury Lamb, except the one on page 55, but including the front cover. The county map is by Robert Dizon.

Ordnance Survey grid references

Although information on how to reach many of the places described in this book by car is given in the text, National Grid References are also included in many instances, particularly for the harder-to-find places in chapters 3, 4 and 8, for the benefit of those readers who have the Ordnance Survey 1:50,000 Landranger maps of the area. The references are stated as a Landranger sheet number followed by the 100 km National Grid square and the six-figure reference.

To locate a site by means of the grid references, proceed as in the following example: Brill Windmill (OS 165: SP 652142). Take the OS Landranger map sheet 165 ('Aylesbury, Leighton Buzzard and District'). The grid numbers are printed in blue around the edges of the map. In more recently produced maps these numbers are repeated at 10 km intervals throughout the map, so that it is not necessary to open it out completely.) Read off these numbers from the left along the top edge of the map until you come to 65, denoting a vertical grid line, then estimate two-tenths of the distance to vertical line 66 and envisage an imaginary vertical grid line 65.2 at this point. Next look at the grid numbers at one side of the map (either side will do) and read *upwards* until you find the horizontal grid line 14. Estimate two-tenths of the distance to the next horizontal line above (i.e. 15), and so envisage an imaginary horizontal line across the map at 14.2. Follow this imaginary line across the map until it crosses the imaginary vertical line 65.2. At the intersection of these two lines you will find Brill Windmill.

The Ordnance Survey Landranger maps which cover Buckinghamshire are sheets 152, 165, 175 and 176.

Cover: *Claydon House, Middle Claydon, home of the Verneys since the seventeenth century.*

Contents

4

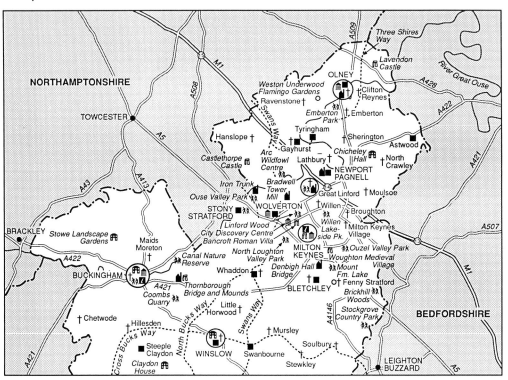

NORTHAMPTONSHIRE

TOWCESTER

BRACKLEY

BEDFORDSHIRE

Three Shires Way

Lavendon Castle

OLNEY

Weston Underwood
Flamingo Gardens

Clifton Reynes

Ravenstone †

Emberton Park

† Emberton

Tyringham

Sherington

Hanslope †

Astwood

Gayhurst

Chicheley Hall

North Crawley

Castlethorpe Castle

Arc Wildfowl Centre

Lathbury †

NEWPORT PAGNELL

Iron Trunk

Bradwell Tower Mill

Great Linford

† Moulsoe

Ouse Valley Park

WOLVERTON

† Willen

† Broughton

STONY STRATFORD

Linford Wood

Willen Lake-side Pk.

Milton Keynes Village

City Discovery Centre

Bancroft Roman Villa

MILTON KEYNES

Ouzel Valley Park

Woughton Medieval Village

Stowe Landscape Gardens

Maids Moreton

Canal Nature Reserve

North Loughton Valley Park

Denbigh Hall Bridge

† Mount Fm. Lake

BUCKINGHAM

Whaddon

BLETCHLEY

O † Fenny Stratford

A421

Thornborough Bridge and Mounds

Brickhill Woods

Coombs Quarry

Little Horwood

Stockgrove Country Park

† Chetwode

Hillesden

† Mursley

Soulbury †

Steeple Claydon

WINSLOW

Swanbourne

Stewkley

LEIGHTON BUZZARD

Claydon House

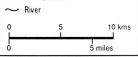

PLACES TO VISIT IN BUCKINGHAMSHIRE

- ■ Town or village (chapter 2)
- ▣ Town or village with information centre (chapters 2 and 12)
- 𝄃𝄃 Countryside (chapter 3)
- 🏛 Ancient monument (chapter 4)
- † Church (chapter 5)
- 🏛 Historic building or garden (chapter 6)
- 🏛 Museum (chapter 7)
- ⚒ Industrial archaeology (chapter 8)
- O Other place to visit (chapter 9)
- ---- Long-distance footpath or bridleway (chapter 3)
- ═ Principal road
- ～ River

0   5   10 kms

0   5 miles

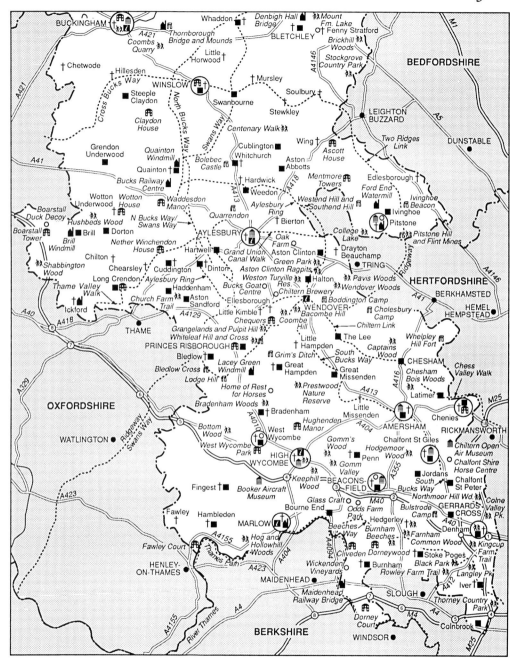

BUCKINGHAM
A421
Coombs
Quarry
Thornborough
Bridge and Mounds
Whaddon
Denbigh Hall
Bridge
Mount
Fm. Lake
Fenny Stratford
BLETCHLEY
A4146
Brickhill
Woods
Stockgrove
Country Park
BEDFORDSHIRE

† Chetwode
Hillesden
Cross Bucks Way
Little
Horwood
WINSLOW
Steeple
Claydon
Claydon
House
Swanbourne
Stewkley
Mursley
Soulbury †
LEIGHTON
BUZZARD
A5
DUNSTABLE

North Bucks Way
Swans Way
Centenary Walk
Cublington
Whitchurch
Wing †
Ascott
House
Two Ridges
Link

A41
Grendon
Underwood
Quainton
Windmill
Quainton †
Bolebec
Castle
Aston
Abbotts
Mentmore
Towers
Edlesborough †
Ford End
Watermill
Ivinghoe
Beacon

Bucks Railway
Centre
Hardwick †
A4413
Weedon †
A418
Westend Hill and
Southend Hill
Ivinghoe
Pitstone

Wotton
Underwood
Wotton
House
Waddesdon
Manor
Aylesbury
Ring
Pitstone Hill
and Flint Mines

Boarstall
Duck Decoy
Rushbeds Wood
N Bucks Way/
Swans Way
Quarrendon
Bierton †
College
Lake

Boarstall
Tower
Dorton
Brill
Nether Winchendon
House
AYLESBURY
Oak
Farm
Aston Clinton
Drayton
Beauchamp †

Brill
Windmill
Chilton †
Hartwell †
Grand Union
Canal Walk
Green Park
Aston Clinton Ragpits
TRING

Ridgeway
Shabbington
Wood
Chearsley †
Cuddington
Dinton †
Weston Turville
Res.
Halton
Pavis Woods
Wendover Woods
HERTFORDSHIRE

Thame Valley
Walk
Long Crendon
Aylesbury Ring
Haddenham
Bucks Goat
Centre
Chiltern Brewery
Boddington Camp
BERKHAMSTED

Ickford
Church Farm
Trail
Aston
Sandford
Eliesborough †
Little Kimble †
WENDOVER
Bacombe
Hill
Cholesbury
Camp
HEMEL
HEMPSTEAD

A40
A418
THAME
A4129
Chequers
Coombe
Hill
Chiltern Link

Grangelands and Pulpit Hill
Whiteleaf Hill and Cross
PRINCES RISBOROUGH
Little
Hampden
The Lee
Whelpley
Hill Fort
Chess
Valley Walk

Bledlow †
Lacey Green
Windmill
Grim's Ditch
South
Bucks Way
Captains
Wood
CHESHAM
Chesham
Bois Woods

Bledlow Cross
Lodge Hill
Home of Rest
for Horses
Great
Hampden †
Great
Missenden
A416
Latimer †

Bradenham Woods
Prestwood
Nature
Reserve
Little
Missenden
A413
Chenies

OXFORDSHIRE
Ridgeway
Swans Way
Bottom
Wood
Bradenham †
Hughenden
Manor
A404
AMERSHAM
RICKMANSWORTH
M25

WATLINGTON
West Wycombe
Park
West
Wycombe
HIGH
WYCOMBE
Gomm's
Wood
Penn †
Hodgemoor
Wood
Chalfont St Giles
Chiltern Open
Air Museum

A423
Fingest †
Booker Aircraft
Museum
Keephill
Wood
Gomm
Valley
BEACONS-
FIELD
A355
Jordans
South
Bucks Way
Chalfont Shire
Horse Centre
Chalfont
St Peter

Fawley †
Hambleden
Glass Craft
Bourne End
Odds Farm
Park
Hedgerley †
Bulstrode
Camp
Northmoor Hill Wd.
GERRARDS
CROSS
Colne
Valley
Pk.

Fawley Court
MARLOW
Hog and
Hollowhill
Woods
A404
Beeches
Way
Cliveden
Burnham
Beeches
Dorneywood
Farnham
Common Wood
A40
Denham
Kingcup
Farm
Trail

HENLEY-
ON-THAMES
Thames Path
A4155
A423
Wickenden
Vineyards
Burnham
Stoke Poges
Black Park
Rowley Farm Trail
Langley Pk
Iver †

MAIDENHEAD
Maidenhead
Railway Bridge
SLOUGH
Thorney Country
Park

A4155
River Thames
A4
Dorney
Court
M4
A4
Colnbrook
M25

BERKSHIRE
WINDSOR

Preface

Welcome to the Shire County Guide to Buckinghamshire, one of over thirty such books, written and designed to enable you to organise your time in the county well.

The Shire County Guides fill the need for a compact, accurate and thorough guide to each county so that visitors can plan a half-day excursion or a whole week's stay to best advantage. Residents, too, will find the guides a handy and reliable reference to the places of interest in their area.

Travelling British roads can be time consuming, and the County Guides will ensure that you need not inadvertently miss any interesting feature in a locality, that you do not accidentally bypass a new museum or an outstanding church, that you can find an attractive place to picnic, and that you will appreciate the history and the buildings of the towns or villages in which you stop.

This book has been arranged in special interest chapters, such as the countryside, historic buildings or ancient monuments, and all these places of interest are located on the map on pages 4-5. Use the map either for an overview to decide which area has most to interest you, or to help you enjoy your immediate neighbourhood. Then refer to the nearest town or village in chapter 2 to see, at a glance, what special features or attractions each community contains or is near. The subsequent chapters enable readers with a particular interest to find immediately those places of importance to them, while the cross-referencing under 'Towns and Villages' assists readers with wider tastes to select how best to spend their time.

1
The Buckinghamshire landscape

Buckinghamshire is one of the smaller English counties. It is just over 50 miles (80 km) from north to south and, at its widest point, 27 miles (43 km) from west to east although its width is generally less than 20 miles (32 km). Historically the county covered 479,358 acres (193,966 hectares) but since boundary changes in 1974 it has embraced 465,260 acres (188,290 hectares).

The transfer of a number of southern parishes to Berkshire in 1974 (Chalvey, Cippenham, Datchet, Eton, Horton, Langley Marsh, Slough and Wraysbury) accentuated the curious shape of the county by moving the boundary away from the river Thames. Although changes in the county boundaries are not without precedent, it was an artificial division, reflected in this guide by the omission of those parishes transferred. Yet Buckinghamshire as a whole is an artificial creation, albeit one that dates from the tenth century AD, whose boundaries follow few natural features. In AD 914 King Edward the Elder ordered the construction of two fortresses on the river Ouse at Buckingham in preparation for his reconquest of the Danelaw; what became Buckinghamshire was the area designated as the territorial basis for their maintenance.

Geology

As a result of these circumstances, the county cuts across geological features, which lie generally in a series of strata running south-west to north-east. A distinct contrast is found, therefore, between the northern and southern halves of the county. At the northern extremity oolite limestones, the oldest geological strata apparent, give way to the valley of the Ouse, more properly the Great or Bedford Ouse, into which flows the Ousel at Newport Pagnell. The Ouse valley itself consists of Middle Jurassic sands, clays and limestones which are then overlaid by Oxford clays, producing the gently undulating countryside around the Claydons and the city of Milton Keynes. Kimmeridge clays, to which the Oxford clays yield, are first overlaid by outcrops of Portland and Purbeck limestones resulting in the steep hills around such villages as Brill, the Winchendons, Quainton, Pitchcott, Whitchurch and the Brickhills. To the south of these outcrops, however, the Kimmeridge clays have produced the low rich pastures of the Vale of Aylesbury, cut by the river Thame and its tributaries flowing westwards to a confluence with the Thames in Oxfordshire. Gault clay forms the southern edge of the Vale as the land rises abruptly to the chalk escarpment of the Chilterns. The Chilterns are in themselves very varied with the high open northern spaces of Coombe Hill and Ivinghoe Beacon contrasting with the heavily wooded Wendover Woods. The Chiltern plateau is similarly varied with numerous differing surface deposits such as clay-with-flints. It is also deeply eroded with valleys, three of which have significant streams: the Wye, flowing directly into the Thames, and the Chess and the Misbourne, flowing into the Colne, a tributary of the Thames. The valley of the Colne is a mixture of Reading Beds, London clays and river gravels.

Forest and vale

The varied geological structure has determined that the county's flora is also diverse although the present appearance of the Buckinghamshire landscape owes all to the way in which man has shaped it over the centuries. Buckinghamshire was once far more heavily wooded with a wider variety of trees than the

Isaac D'Israeli's monument near Downley.

beech with which it is now chiefly associated. Most of the traces of the larger forests in the north of the county have long since disappeared, but comparatively recently in terms of the development of the landscape. The great forest of Bernwood, comprising over 8000 acres (3200 hectares) around Brill, Oakley and Boarstall in the thirteenth century, was disafforested only in the seventeenth century. Perhaps the most celebrated of the many beechwoods in the Chilterns and Chiltern plateau is Burnham Beeches. However, the beech has become predominant only since the eighteenth century as arable land became forested anew and other varieties of tree became displaced. Even the often grotesque appearance of the trees in Burnham Beeches is a result of the constant pollarding by man between the sixteenth and nineteenth centuries. Similarly, the elm that was one of the main features of the Vale of Aylesbury, until devastated by Dutch elm disease in the 1970s, was introduced by man. The rich texture of field and hedgerow in the Vale is obvious from any vantage point on the Chiltern scarp or from that road between Whitchurch and Oving described by Sir Colin Buchanan as 'as beautiful a road (for its views) as any I know in the Home Counties'. It has been described memorably by A. G.

MacDonnell in *England, Their England* and painted lovingly by Rex Whistler. Yet the Vale's present appearance is merely the result of the break-up of the medieval landscape by a process of steady enclosure from the fourteenth to the early nineteenth century. In that time, too, large numbers of former settlements totally disappeared so that there are fewer villages than might otherwise have been the case.

Settlement patterns

In short, the Buckinghamshire landscape reflects the influence of the hand of man from earliest times although the geological structure, in itself, has shaped that influence. Archaeology has revealed evidence of palaeolithic man in the Thames and Ouse valleys and of mesolithic man in the Colne valley and the Chilterns. The first large remains visible are round barrows and ring-ditches of the neolithic or bronze age while, at Ivinghoe Beacon, there is evidence of the transition between bronze and iron age, the latter characterised by the hillforts found along the scarp of the Chilterns. But such early settlement was determined by the natural communications corridors provided by the river valleys and the lower scarp, along which wound the ancient trackways of the Lower and Upper Icknield Way and the Ridgeway. In the period of Roman occupation Buckinghamshire was quite densely settled in relation to an elaborate road network, of which the chief reminders are the course of Watling Street (now the A5) and Akeman Street (now the A41). Indeed, the county has always been a focus for communication routes between north and south, the Wendover and Risborough gaps of the Chilterns being especially important in this regard. The important geographical position of Buckinghamshire has continued to shape development, canals and railways being pushed through the landscape in the nineteenth century in much the same way that the M1, M4, M25 and M40 motorways have appeared in the twentieth century.

Agriculture and industry

Geology also determined that Buckinghamshire would be primarily an agricultural county and so it has largely remained. There was long a distinction between pastoral and dairying activities in the Vale of Aylesbury and the north and the arable farming predominant in the Chilterns and the south. However, during the two world wars more land was brought under the plough and since the

Second World War arable production has been encouraged. Thus the former distinction has become blurred. Traditionally, any industry that existed was also based upon the land and the cottage. In the eighteenth and nineteenth centuries the greatest rural industries were straw plait and lacemaking. The latter was well established by the sixteenth century and was recorded as being of supreme importance by every observer of the county from Fuller in 1660 to Defoe in 1708 and Priest in 1813. Similarly, the importance of duck-rearing around Aylesbury is well-known. The only occupations that could be called extraction industries were brickmaking, which was particularly important around Brill between the thirteenth and nineteenth centuries, and chairmaking in the Chilterns. A purely localised industry was the needlemaking carried on at Long Crendon from the sixteenth century until 1862. As late as the First World War, the only large industrial concerns were the furniture factories of High Wycombe, the railway works established at Wolverton in the mid nineteenth century, and printing works in Aylesbury and Wolverton. Development since the First World War has been primarily light industry, the trading estate created at Slough (now in Berkshire) in

The Vale of Aylesbury from Halton.

1920 being the forerunner of this kind of industrial expansion.

Architecture

Buckinghamshire not only lacked minerals that could be readily exploited industrially, but much of the county also lacked building stone, although in the north there are many stone buildings, some built from local stone. Consequently stone had to be imported from neighbouring counties and the predominant building material in the past was brick within a timber frame. That and the absence of any especially large town may explain the lack of castles, cathedrals and significant monastic foundations, although there are sites of Norman motte and bailey castles and a handful of monastic survivals. In some areas local variations in building material occur such as the flint prevalent in the Chilterns and the unique local wichert employed for building in the villages of Cuddington, Lower Winchendon and Haddenham. Wichert derives from a chalky marl, found only in those localities, which was soaked in water and mixed with chopped straw to be moulded in layers to form walls. Stone rubble footings were necessary to protect the structure from damp and walls were topped with tile or thatch and rendered with rough-cast or plaster to keep out the rain. At Haddenham in particular there are extensive wichert walls, which give the village a curiously continental appearance.

The county makes up for its lack of medieval buildings, other than its churches, in its secular buildings dating from the sixteenth to eighteenth centuries. Of houses of the earliest period, Chenies Manor and Dorney Court are fine examples, although they were often added to or altered in subsequent years. Of the seventeenth century, Dorton House may stand as representative while eighteenth-century taste is evident at Claydon House, West Wycombe Park and Stowe School. Moreover, these great houses are often set amongst landscaped grounds laid out by such masters of the art as 'Capability' Brown and Humphry Repton. Of a later period of architecture, the county has the magnificent Victorian mansions built for the Rothschilds such as Ascott House, Mentmore Towers and Waddesdon Manor.

Indeed, only one English county has more National Trust properties open to the public while, at Long Crendon, Buckinghamshire also has one of the first buildings ever acquired by the Trust.

A county's essence

The great houses, the county's museums and many of its churches and villages have constant reminders of historical figures of national importance. Benjamin Disraeli, a resident of Buckinghamshire, remarked that 'there is something in the air of Bucks favourable to political knowledge and vigour', and the county has associations with some celebrated politicians of independent mind: Edmund Burke, John Wilkes, John Hampden and the Grenvilles of Stowe among them. Its earlier liberal political tradition was also reflected in the spread of religious dissent, of which William Penn, the Quaker, is one of the foremost representatives. There are also many literary associations with such writers as John Milton, Thomas Gray and William Cowper.

That Buckinghamshire should inspire poetry is not surprising for it has always had a great propensity to induce loyalty and love both among those born in the county and those who have become its residents. However, it is the pressure of that population that has most threatened the survival of the county's countryside. The proximity to London and the major communications routes has seen the almost inexorable advance of suburbia in the south of the county while, in 1967, much of north-eastern Buckinghamshire was designated as the site of the new city of Milton Keynes. Already the county has one of the fastest growing populations in England, its numbers increasing from 476,251 in the 1971 census to 632,487 in that of 1991. Fortunately, despite some of its more experimental architecture, some care has been taken to preserve the landscape in and around Milton Keynes. But few of the larger towns in the county have survived altogether the attention of the planners and developers and the county seems destined to remain under constant threat.

The Buckinghamshire landscape has

The island temple in West Wycombe Park.

evolved as a result of the continuing interaction of many factors over the course of the centuries. Change is inevitable but, in the past, it was most often gradual rather than accelerated and it somehow preserved the quintessential nature of the Buckinghamshire countryside. Fortunately, there are still many unspoilt corners of the county where the visitor can recapture for a moment a world largely lost. It is to be hoped that future generations will be able to experience that same unspoilt Buckinghamshire countryside.

2
Towns and villages

Amersham

Early closing Thursday; market days Tuesday and Friday.

With the completion of the bypass, Amersham has to some extent regained the atmosphere of an eighteenth-century coaching town nestled in the valley of the Misbourne. However, although the High Street has a number of attractive buildings, the effect to the east of the Town or Market Hall is rather spoiled by the presence of the gasholder and the large supermarket built in the early 1990s. The Market Hall itself was built for the Drake family of Shardeloes in 1682 and is the most conspicuous feature of the High Street. On the south side, the Crown hotel has a sixteenth-century interior while Elmodesham House is early eighteenth-century and Number 47 is fifteenth-century; Number 61 is seventeenth-century and has a ground-floor room with seventeenth-century wall paintings of the Nine Worthies. Also on the south side of the High Street towards Aylesbury may be found the Drake Almshouses of 1657 and the seventeenth-century Little Shardeloes. On the north side, The Mill is late seventeenth-century, as is The Gables. The church of St Mary may be found in Church Street leading off High Street and the Baptist chapel behind the King's Arms. In Whielden Street is the Friends' Meeting House and the Amersham Museum is in the High Street.

The remainder of the old town and Amersham-on-the-Hill are of less interest except the Martyrs' Memorial, which can be reached from a footpath in the cemetery. It was erected in 1931 by the Protestant Alliance to mark the spot where one Protestant was burned at the stake in 1506 and a further six in 1521. East of Station Road is A. D. Connell's concrete 'International style' house of 1931, called High and Over. Visible on its hill to the south of the main road to Aylesbury lies Shardeloes, now luxury flats but built as a mansion for the Drakes by Stiff Leadbetter between 1758 and 1766, with later alterations by Robert Adam and grounds by Repton.

Church of St Mary, page 57; **Amersham Museum**, page 79.

In the locality: Chesham Bois Woods, page 45; Hodgemoor Wood, page 48; Little Missenden church, page 65; Chenies Manor House, page 70; Milton's Cottage, page 82; Chiltern Open Air Museum, page 79. See also Chalfont St Giles, page 18; Chesham, page 19; and Latimer, page 33.

Ashley Green
Whelpley Hill Fort, page 56.

Aston Abbotts

This hilltop village is notable primarily for the Abbey, the home of James Clark Ross, the polar explorer and discoverer of the magnetic pole, who is buried in the churchyard of St James and commemorated by a stained glass window. In the Second World War the Abbey was the home of the Czech government in exile, whose president, Eduard Benes, presented the brick bus shelter on the A418 to the village after the war.

Aston Clinton

Site of the demolished mansion of Sir Anthony de Rothschild (see page 95), Aston Clinton is still visibly a Rothschild village. Two schools were built close to the church by Gotto of Tring for de Rothschild in 1856 and 1862 respectively (the former has been demolished), while the Anthony Hall was erected in 1884 as a memorial to Sir Anthony's wife. Evelyn Waugh once taught at a preparatory school in the village and wrote part of *Decline and Fall* there.

Aston Clinton Ragpits, page 44; **Green Park**, page 48.

In the locality: Pavis Woods, page 50. See also Halton, page 27.

Amersham town hall.

Aston Sandford

Essentially a hamlet of Haddenham, Aston Sandford is notable for one of the few domestic buildings designed by George Gilbert Scott (see page 57) – the Manor. Scott's grandfather, the Reverend Thomas Scott, who succeeded John Newton as curate at Olney, was rector here from 1800 to 1821. He was a founder of the Church Missionary Society and author of *The Force of Truth.*

See also Haddenham, page 27.

Astwood

Of interest here is Dove House, now converted into a private residence but formerly a late seventeenth-century dovecote capable of accommodating three hundred nests. It is all that remains of Astwoodbury House, a mansion considered by the antiquarian Browne Willis to be one of the finest in the county but which was demolished in 1799.

In the locality: Chicheley Hall, page 71; and churches at North Crawley, page 66; and Sherington, page 67.

Aylesbury

Early closing Thursday; market days Wednesday, Friday and Saturday.

On a slight rise most evident around the church of St Mary at the heart of the Vale, Aylesbury has been Buckinghamshire's county town since the sixteenth century but the character of the old town was all but destroyed by development in the 1960s. The dominating eleven-storey County Offices of 1966 are a suitable illustration of the harm that has been done. Fortunately, traces of a more elegant past have survived. The 1960s shopping complex of Friars Square, into which the visitor emerges from the multistorey car park, for example, did not completely destroy the atmosphere of the Market Square beyond and has now been replaced by a more attractive shopping area. Moreover, the Market Square has been substantially pedestrianised. The old County Hall forms the south side of the square together with the Corn Exchange of 1865. Built by Thomas Harris, with the possible assistance of Sir

John Vanbrugh, between 1723 and 1740, the County Hall contains an eighteenth-century courtroom, which was used for the trial of the Great Train Robbers and restored to its original form after a fire in 1970. The prominent clock-tower in the Market Square dates from 1876. Some indication of the eighteenth-century appearance of the square may be derived from a consideration of surviving buildings along the north side of the square while an alley there opens on to the façade of the fifteenth-century King's Head, owned by the National Trust. The large contemporary mullioned window contains the arms of King Henry VI and Margaret of Anjou and presumably commemorates their marriage in 1445.

From the King's Head in the north-west corner of the square, Market Street may be followed almost immediately into Temple Street, leading to Temple Square and Church Street. While Temple Square still has the air of the eighteenth century, Church Street has two refronted fifteenth-century houses opposite the County Museum.

Beyond the museum lies the church of St Mary, standing in St Mary's Square. Pebble Lane may be followed past a restored water pump to Kingsbury Square and the Market Square while Parson's Fee leads past a group of seventeenth- and eighteenth-century houses and the eighteenth-century Prebendal House, home of John Wilkes (see page 97), into Castle Street, Rickford's Hill and back to Temple Square.

On the outskirts of the town is Stoke Mandeville Hospital, renowned for treatment of spinal injuries and the site of the international Paraplegic Games.

Grand Union Canal – Aylesbury Arm Walk, page 47; **Buckinghamshire County Museum**, page 79; **Church of St Mary**, page 57.

In the locality: Coombe Hill, page 47; Wendover Woods, page 52; Quarrendon, page 56; Nether Winchendon House, page 74; Buckinghamshire Railway Centre, page 87; Bucks Goat Centre, page 91; Oak Farm Rare Breeds Park, page 92. See also Cublington, page 22; Cuddington, page 22; Dinton, page 22; Haddenham, page 27; Halton, page 27; Quainton, page 38; Weedon,

Temple Square, Aylesbury.

page 40; Wendover, page 40; and Whitchurch, page 42.

Beaconsfield
Early closing Wednesday; market day Tuesday.

The heart of Old Beaconsfield is London End, one of four such 'Ends'. It still shows traces of the days when the town was an important staging post on the London to Oxford road. The privately owned Burke's Lodge on the south side of London End has a window, formerly part of the Crown, from which coach drivers could be served and the gates between Burke's Lodge and Roche House once opened into the inn courtyard. The Swan is sixteenth-century in origin while the Royal Saracen's Head hides a sixteenth-century interior behind nineteenth-century mock Tudor. On the opposite side of London End, the former King's Head is a sixteenth-century inn remodelled in the early eighteenth century.

Windsor End leads to Hall Barn, built for Edmund Waller (see page 96) between 1675 and 1699 and now restored to its original appearance through the removal of later additions by Lord Burnham between 1969 and 1972. The Hall Barn estate, which is not open to the public, is also notable for its landscaped grounds, begun for Waller in the seventeenth century and representing one of the earliest such gardens in England.

At the junction of Windsor End and Wycombe End is the church of St Mary and All Saints with its memories of Waller and Edmund Burke (see page 97). Behind the church are the early sixteenth-century Old Rectory and Capel's House.

Apart from Waller and Burke, Beaconsfield has many other literary associations. G. K. Chesterton lived at Top Meadow on the corner of Grove Road off Station Road from 1909 to 1935 and is commemorated by a bust in the White Hart. Robert Frost lived at The Bungalow in Reynolds Road from 1912 to 1915 while William Hickey lived at Little Hall Barn in Windsor End. Enid Blyton was also a resident.

Other attractions include the Royal Army Educational Corps Museum in the grounds of the eighteenth-century Wilton Park off Park Lane and, in the twentieth-century new town, the famous model village of Bekonscot.

Church of St Mary and All Saints, page 58; **Royal Army Educational Corps Museum**, page 79; **Bekonscot Model Village**, page 91.

In the locality: Burnham Beeches, page 45; Church Wood Nature Reserve, page 46; Bulstrode Camp, page 54. See also Gerrards Cross, page 26; Jordans, page 31; and Penn, page 37.

Bierton
Church of St James, page 58.

Bledlow
Backed by Wain Hill, upon which stand the remains of an ancient barrow known as the Cop, the village also lies across the wooded ravine of the Lyde, through which flows one of the tributaries of the Thame. The eighteenth-century manor house is owned by the former Foreign Secretary, Lord Carrington. The house itself is not open to the public but a water garden laid out by the Carringtons is open to visitors all year round.

Bledlow Cross, page 54; **Church of Holy Trinity**, page 58.

Bletchley
Early closing Wednesday; market days Thursday and Saturday.

Bletchley has expanded greatly since the 1950s and it is the largest of the three towns (the others being Stony Stratford and Wolverton) incorporated into the city of Milton Keynes. Consequently, it is now of little interest, the most notable older feature being Bletchley Park, now in the hands of British Telecom but known for its vital role in cryptography and intelligence during the Second World War when it was the Government Code and Cypher School employing over twelve thousand people. It is anticipated that a museum of cryptography and computing will be opened, featuring a reconstruction of the world's first computer, Colossus, as well as taking visitors through the whole 'Ultra' process of receiving and decoding intercepted German signals. (For more information, contact: The Bletchley Park Trust, Suite 8,

Bradenham church and manor house.

Denbigh House, Denbigh Road, Bletchley, Milton Keynes MK1 1YP. Telephone: 01908 640404 or 274381.) Modern architecture includes the Brunel Shopping Centre of 1973, the Leisure Centre and Jennie Lee Theatre.

Church of St Mary, page 58; **Mount Farm Lake**, page 49.

In the locality: Fenny Lodge Gallery, page 91; Woughton Medieval Village, page 56. See also Fenny Stratford, page 26, and Milton Keynes, page 35.

Boarstall

Boarstall Tower, page 70; Boarstall Duck Decoy, page 91.

Bourne End

Bourne End experienced a late growth as a result of the popularity of boating in Victorian England. Cores End House dates from the early eighteenth century but the rest of the town is mainly Victorian villas and later bungalows. Abbots Brook estate is a pleasant 1890s development of half-timbered houses along a trout stream. The best of Bourne End is the view across the river Thames; the river also provides the town with its annual sailing week (see page 100).

Bow Brickhill

Brickhill Woods, page 45.

Bradenham

Bradenham has been largely owned by the National Trust since 1956. Apart from the church of St Botolph and its surrounding woods, the village is also characterised by the late seventeenth-century manor, which was the home of Isaac D'Israeli. He was the father of Benjamin Disraeli (see page 94) and is buried in the church.

Bradenham Woods, page 45; **Church of St Botolph**, page 58.

Brill

Over 600 feet (180 metres) above sea level, Brill has a commanding view of the surrounding countryside, best seen from the Common. It was the site of a former palace of Edward the Confessor and the early Norman kings and was fortified by the Royalists from Oxford during the Civil War. There is now some confusion between the earthwork remains of these former uses and old clay workings. The square has some seventeenth- and eighteenth-century features while the Manor House originally dates from the sixteenth century. Tram Hill

Parsons Fee, Aylesbury, leads to St Mary's church.

The Old Rectory by Beaconsfield church.

was the site of the terminus of the Brill Tramway from Quainton Road station, closed in 1935.
Brill Windmill, page 87.

Broughton (near Aylesbury)
Oak Farm Rare Breeds Park, page 92.

Broughton (near Milton Keynes)
Church of St Lawrence, page 58.

Buckingham
Early closing Thursday; market days
Tuesday and Saturday.
Buckingham is an ancient town mentioned in
the Anglo-Saxon Chronicle and the site of the
two fortresses constructed by King Edward
the Elder in AD 914, the strategic significance of the view over town and surrounding
countryside from Castle Hill being evident. It
remained the county town until the sixteenth
century, when the status was lost to Aylesbury, although temporarily successful efforts
were made to restore the county assizes during the eighteenth century. Much of the town
dates from the eighteenth century, when extensive rebuilding was necessary after a disastrous fire in 1725. The church of St Peter
and St Paul was also rebuilt in the eighteenth
century. Nevertheless, the late eighteenth-
century front of the Town Hall, topped by the
swan of the county's arms, conceals a late
seventeenth-century interior. Similarly, the
eighteenth-century façade of Castle House in
West Street conceals an older house in which
Queen Catharine of Aragon was entertained
in 1514 , and King Charles I during the Civil
War. Off Market Hill, too, is the ancient
Chantry Chapel.
   The mock castellations of the Old Gaol at
the opposite end of Market Square from the
Town Hall are an eighteenth-century creation, it having been erected for Lord Cobham
of Stowe in 1748 as part of the attempt to
have the assizes relocated here; George
Gilbert Scott remodelled the south front in
1839. The Old Gaol is now a museum.
   There are a number of other interesting
features outside the Market Square. In
Chandos Road, The Firs is notable for being
built of forest marble, a locally worked lime-

stone, in the early nineteenth century, while
there are both the old militia barracks built in
1802 in West Street and old yeomanry barracks and Yeomanry House, now occupied
by the University of Buckingham, in Hunter
Street. A town trail is available, prepared by
the Buckingham Society.
   Buckingham Railway Walk, page 45; **Canal Nature Reserve**, page 45; **Church of St
Peter and St Paul**, page 59; **Chantry Chapel**,
page 70; **Stowe Landscape Gardens**, page
75; **The Old Gaol Museum**, page 79.
   *In the locality: Coombs Quarry, page 47;
Thornborough Mounds, page 56;
Thornborough Bridge, page 90; church at
Maids Moreton, page 65.*

Burnham
A nunnery occupies the restored remains of
the thirteenth-century Augustinian Burnham
Abbey while Huntercombe Manor retains
some fourteenth-century features despite re-
modelling in the nineteenth century. Once
owned by the Evelyn family, Huntercombe
was visited by the diarist John Evelyn in
1679. East Burnham Cottage is associated
with Sheridan.
   Burnham Beeches, page 45; **Church of St
Peter**, page 59; **Dorneywood Garden**, page 72.

Castlethorpe
Castlethorpe Castle, page 54.

Chalfont St Giles
Best known for Milton's Cottage, the village
also has associations with Captain James
Cook. The Vache, to the north-east, and now
owned by the British Coal Corporation, came
into the possession of Admiral Sir Hugh
Palliser in 1777. Palliser had been Cook's
patron and, just as Cook named a Pacific
island Ile Vache after Palliser's home, Palliser
had a commemorative arch erected to Cook
in 1785. Dibden Hill to the south was the site
of a socialist colony founded by the Frenchman P. H. J. Baume in 1846. The church of St
Giles is of interest, while the Chiltern Open
Air Museum is close to the village.
   Hodgemoor Wood, page 48; **Church of
St Giles**, page 59; **Chiltern Open Air Museum**, page 79; **Milton's Cottage**, page 82;

The Bury, Chesham.

Chalfont Shire Horse Centre, page 91.

Chalfont St Peter

The village is notable for Chalfont House, a mid eighteenth-century Gothic creation by John Chute for General Charles Churchill which was later altered by Anthony Salvin in 1836. The Grange is on the site of the Quaker home of the Penningtons. Outside the Chalfont Epileptic Colony, opened in 1895, is a 60 foot (18 metre) high obelisk dated 1785 and probably utilised as a signpost to Sir Henry Gott's Newland Park although ostensibly commemorating the killing of a stag by King George III.

Chearsley
Church of St Nicholas, page 59.

Cheddington
Westend Hill and Southend Hill, page 56.

Chenies

Above the wooded valley of the Chess, Chenies is essentially a mid-Victorian model village laid out by the Bedford Estate: the family tombs of the Russells are in the celebrated Bedford Chapel of the church of St Michael. However, the manor house is older and the Baptist chapel is of 1778.

Chenies Manor House, page 70; **Church of St Michael**, page 60.

Chesham

Although this small town has suffered from modern development, some attractive buildings remain around the church. Off Church Street is The Bury, built for William Lowndes, the Secretary to the Treasury, in 1712. In the High Street, from which the Market Hall was removed in the 1960s, the George has early eighteenth-century wall paintings while next door, Arthur Liberty, founder of the London store, once had a draper's shop. To the west of the town lie Great Hundridge Manor, built in 1696, and a thirteenth-century flint chapel associated with a former house on the same site.

Captains Wood, page 45.

In the locality: Chesham Bois Woods, page

Wild orchids in flower on Pulpit Hill near Great Kimble.

Opposite: *The water garden at Bledlow is open for the enjoyment of the villagers.*

At College Lake Wildlife Centre, Pitstone, poppies, corn cockle and cornflowers grow among the crops in traditionally cultivated plots.

45; *Whelpley Hill Fort, page 56. See also Amersham, page 12.*

Chesham Bois
Chesham Bois Woods, page 45.

Chetwode
Church of St Mary and St Nicholas, page 60.

Chicheley
Chicheley Hall, page 71.

Chilton
Church of St Mary, page 60.

Cholesbury
Cholesbury Camp, page 55.

Clifton Reynes
Church of St Mary, page 60.

Colnbrook
Once an important staging post on the old Bath Road, the inns of Colnbrook are of great historic interest. The future Queen Elizabeth I stayed at the George in 1558 en route to captivity at Hampton Court during her sis-ter's reign. The Ostrich was the scene of a series of seventeenth-century .murders (see page 99). Colnbrook was also where King Edward III met the Black Prince in 1355 when the latter returned with the king of France as his prisoner after the battle of Poitiers. Cox's Orange Pippin was first grown and sent to market in England in 1825 at Colnbrook Lawn.

Cublington
The remains of a Norman motte and bailey known as the Beacon can be found to the west of the church while to the north-west are the eighteenth-century stable block and grain store of a former manor house. A spinney commemorates the successful outcome of the campaign to prevent the siting of the third London airport in the village in April 1971.

Cuddington
Cuddington is one of the county's 'wichert' villages with a prominent church, timber-framed cottages and a village pump. Tyringham House dates from the early seventeenth century. The journalist and historian Chester Wilmot once resided in the village.
Church of St Nicholas, page 60.

Denham village.

'Dinton Castle' folly.

Denham

Apart from its church, Denham has a number of interesting mansions. Denham Place was built for Sir Roger Hill between 1688 and 1701 and has grounds laid out by 'Capability' Brown; it became the home of Lucien and Joseph Bonaparte in exile and later was the home of Lord Vansittart. Denham Court is now mostly of the eighteenth century but, as the seventeenth-century home of the Bowyer family, it was visited by Dryden, who composed his *Ode on St Cecilia's Feast* there. The Savoy, parts of which date back to the fourteenth century, was the home of Sir Oswald Mosley, and his wife Cynthia was buried in the grounds until vandalism compelled the removal of her grave in 1970. On the main A412 lie the former Rank Studios, designed by Walter Gropius and Maxwell Fry in 1936 and associated with the epic films of Sir Alexander Korda.

Church of St Mary, page 60; **Northmoor Hill Wood**, page 50; **Kingcup Farm Trail**, page 49; **Colne Valley Park**, page 46; **Denham Country Park**, page 47.

Dinton

Dinton Hall, a mainly sixteenth-century mansion, is associated with the regicide Simon Mayne. Mayne's secretary, John Bigge, became the 'Dinton Hermit' (see page 99) after his master died in the Tower of London in 1661. Subsequently Dinton Hall came into the possession of the Vanhatten family and 'Dinton Castle', a folly off the main Aylesbury road, was erected for Sir John Vanhatten in 1769 to display his collection of fossils. The church is of interest.

Church of St Peter and St Paul, page 60.

Dorney

Dorney Court, page 72.

Dorton

Dorton House, now a private school, is an H-shaped Jacobean mansion built for Sir John

The spire of Olney church can be seen across one of the lakes at Emberton Park.

Opposite: *Fingest church has a tower with a remarkable twin saddleback roof.*

The village pond at Haddenham.

Dormer between 1596 and 1626. The village was also the site of a spa from 1830 to 1839.

Drayton Beauchamp
Church of St Mary, page 60.

Edlesborough
Church of St Mary, page 61.

Ellesborough
Church of St Peter and St Paul, page 61; Chequers, page 61.

Emberton
Emberton Park, page 47; Church of All Saints, page 61.

Fawley
Church of St Mary, page 61; Fawley Court, page 72.

Fenny Stratford
Church of St Martin, page 62; Denbigh Hall Bridge, page 87; Fenny Lodge Gallery, page 91.

Fingest
Chiefly known for the church of St Bartholomew, Fingest is nonetheless a picturesque village in the Hambleden valley with the remains of the old village pound still to be found in Chequers Lane.
Church of St Bartholomew, page 62.

Gayhurst
Gayhurst has one of the most historic of Buckinghamshire houses, although it is not open to the public. The present Gayhurst House owes much to George Wright, for whom the garden front was remodelled in the eighteenth century and for whom the church was also rebuilt. However, the main front still reflects the house begun for William Mulso in 1597 on the foundations of a still older house. Mulso's work was completed by his son-in-law, Sir Everard Digby, who was executed in 1606 for his part in the Gunpowder Plot. Some of the conspiracy was planned in the house. The grounds were worked upon by both 'Capability' Brown and Humphry Repton.
Church of St Peter, page 62.

Gerrards Cross
Gerrards Cross is a product of the railway age, the parish being created from five neighbouring parishes only in 1861. It enjoyed particularly rapid growth in the early twentieth century and is synonymous with 'Metroland', although the early nineteenth-century frontage of the Bull Hotel testifies to an earlier importance in the coaching age. Bulstrode Park was once the property of Judge Jeffreys and later of the third Duke of Portland (see page 94), although the present house dates from 1862. Bulstrode Park also contains the largest iron age hillfort in the county.
Bulstrode Camp, page 54.

Great Hampden
Great Hampden is not so much a village as a house largely associated with John Hampden (see page 96) and, indeed, many relics associated with him are preserved there. Much of the present house, which is not open to the public, is actually of the eighteenth century but King John's Tower is fourteenth-century in origin and the Brick Parlour remains much as it was when Hampden was supposedly arrested there for non-payment of Ship Money. Grim's Ditch runs through the grounds. John Hampden is commemorated by a monument near Honor End Farm, on the road to Prestwood, one mile (1.6 km) southeast (OS 165: SP 862020).
Grim's Ditch, page 55; **Church of St Mary Magdalene**, page 62.

Great Kimble
Grangelands and Pulpit Hill Nature Reserve, page 48.

Great Linford
Arc Wildfowl Centre, page 44; Great Linford Manor House Park, page 48; Linford Wood, page 49; Great Linford Brick Kilns, page 89; Church of St Andrew, page 62.

Great Missenden
Much of the interest lies along the High Street with its seventeenth- and eighteenth-century buildings. Behind the George Inn lies the former manorial courthouse, dating from the sixteenth century and still in use as such until

Missenden Abbey.

the early twentieth century. The most important building, however, is Missenden Abbey, used as an adult education centre since 1947. Originally founded in 1133 by an Augustinian order, it was remodelled extensively for James Oldham in 1787 and then gothicised for John Ayton in 1806.

In the locality: Prestwood Local Nature Reserve, page 50.

Grendon Underwood

Principally known now as the site of an open prison, the village once lay on the boundaries of the forest of Bernwood. To the east of the church along the main street is Shakespeare Farm, formerly the New or Ship Inn. According to John Aubrey, William Shakespeare stayed at the inn and was inspired by the surroundings and the clientele to write *A Midsummer Night's Dream.*

Haddenham

The principal 'wichert' village in Buckinghamshire, Haddenham is also notable for its reminders of the duck-rearing industry. In the various 'Ends' there are many interesting buildings. To the east of the church, the timber-framed Church Farm has features dating from the fourteenth to the sixteenth century while Grenville Manor, notwithstanding the Victorian origin of its 1569 datestone, does have sixteenth-century features. To the west of the church, Manor Farmhouse has a fifteenth-century barn. In the High Street, the Bone House, built in 1807, is decorated with knucklebones.

Church Farm Trail, page 46.

Halton

A Rothschild village, Halton has many buildings displaying the five arrows of the family crest and still others decorated with plaster plaques of rural scenes. On the post office, for example, there are plaques showing a girl holding fruit, another feeding hens, a harvester, a skater and the Rothschild motto of 'Concord, industry and integrity'. Halton House was built for Baron Alfred de Rothschild (see page 95) in 1884, was used by the army and Royal Flying Corps during the First World War and taken over permanently by the newly formed Royal Air Force when the baron died in 1918.

Boddington Camp Hillfort, page 54.

The Court House at Long Crendon was one of the first buildings acquired by the National Trust.
Opposite: *Autumn colours stand out against the conifers on the slopes of Wendover Woods.*

Hambleden

Hambleden is a picturesque village with access to the river Thames, the weir and the much photographed watermill. The church is also of interest while Kenricks stands on the birthplace of St Thomas of Cantelupe (see page 98). The seventeenth-century Manor House was the birthplace of the seventh Earl of Cardigan, who led the Light Brigade into the 'Valley of Death' at the battle of Balaclava during the Crimean War in 1854.

Church of St Mary, page 62.

Hanslope
Church of St James the Great, page 62.

Hardwick
Church of St Mary, page 62.

Hartwell
Hartwell House, which is now a luxury hotel, is a Jacobean mansion with an eighteenth-

century front and largely remodelled eighteenth-century interior. Occupied by the exiled King Louis XVIII of France from 1807 until his first restoration in 1814, the house also has a significant park, believed to have been laid out by Richard Woods. The bridge over the park lake was formerly an archway from Kew Bridge. Other features are the wall of ammonites constructed in 1855 for the eccentric Dr John Lee and the remains of a stone pylon, executed for Lee by Bonomi in 1840, over the Egyptian Spring on the road to Lower Hartwell.

Hedgerley

Church Wood Nature Reserve, page 46;
Farnham Common Wood, page 47; Church
of St Mary, page 63.

High Wycombe

Early closing Wednesday; market days Tuesday, Friday and Saturday.
Only a few buildings survive to suggest the town that existed before the widespread use of concrete. The large church is a central starting point from which Church Square and Cornmarket may be followed into the High Street. The two most prominent buildings are the Guildhall and Market Hall, both the gift of the Shelburne family (see page 94). The latter was designed by Robert Adam in 1761. Much of the remainder of the High Street has been altered greatly, the Red Lion, associated with Disraeli, being incorporated into Woolworths. Queen Victoria Street and Abbey Way lead to the former Shelburne mansion of Wycombe Abbey at the foot of Marlow Hill. Now a girls' school, the present Wycombe Abbey is the work of James Wyatt and dates from 1795, when the estate was purchased by the Carrington family. The ancient open common of the Rye should also be noted. On the north of the town, Priory Avenue leads to Castle Hill House, now the Wycombe Local History and Chair Museum. Apart from its links with the Shelburnes and with Disraeli, whose Hughenden home lies nearby, High Wycombe was also the location of one of England's first Sunday schools, opened by Hannah Ball in 1769. Above the town, on

Halton House.

Marlow Hill, is the impressive, modern sports centre.

Chairborough Nature Reserve, page 45; **Gomm's Wood**, page 47; **Gomm Valley**, page 47; **Keephill Wood**, page 48; **Church of All Saints**, page 60; **Hughenden Manor**, page 72; **Booker Aircraft Museum**, page 82; **Wycombe Local History and Chair Museum**, page 82.

In the locality: West Wycombe Park, page 78; West Wycombe Caves and Mausoleum, page 93; Bradenham Woods, page 45.

Hillesden

Church of All Saints, page 64.

Hughenden

Hughenden Manor, page 72.

Ickford

Church of St Nicholas, page 64; Ickford
Bridge, page 89.

Iver

Iver's church has interesting monuments and the houses in the village have some interesting associations. Iver Grove, a National Trust property, of which only the exterior and the hall are open by appointment, was built by Sir John Vanbrugh between 1722 and 1724. Coppins, which is also not open to the public, was the home of the Duke of Kent until 1972, while the Victorian architect G. F. Bodley lived at Bridgefoot House and the artists John and Paul Nash at Wood Lane House. The nearby village of **Iver Heath** has Black Park and Langley Park and the 1934 Pinewood film studios.

Thorney Country Park, page 52; **Church of St Peter**, page 64.

In the locality: Black Park, page 44; Langley Park, page 49; Rowley Farm Trail, page 51.

Ivinghoe

An access point for Ivinghoe Beacon and the Ridgeway, the village is grouped around a green. It was supposedly the inspiration for the title of Sir Walter Scott's novel *Ivanhoe*. The village is also of interest to the industrial archaeologist for its watermill and railway cutting.

Ivinghoe Beacon, page 55; **Ford End Watermill**, page 89; **Pitstone Windmill**, page 90.

See also Pitstone, page 37.

Jordans

Meeting House open Mondays and Wednesdays to Sundays; Sunday service at 10.30 a.m. Telephone: 01240 74586.

Left: *The Guildhall from the Market Hall, High Wycombe.*
Right: *'Red Lion', High Street, High Wycombe.*

In steam at the Buckinghamshire Railway Centre, Quainton Road railway station.
Princes Risborough's restored Market Hall.

Owned by the Society of Friends, Jordans has special associations for the Quakers and with William Penn (see page 95). Old Jordans is William Russell's early seventeenth-century farmhouse, in which Penn and other early Quakers held their meetings. The Mayflower Barn, originally the barn of Jordans Farm, is now firmly established as being partly constructed from the timbers of the *Mayflower*. Below the barn is the Meeting House, which was built in 1688, when the passing of the Toleration Act permitted such buildings to be erected, with money left in trust by the widow of another leading Quaker, Isaac Pennington (1616-79). Outside lie the graves of William Penn, his wives Gulielma and Hannah, ten of his sixteen children, Isaac Pennington and Thomas Ellwood (1639-1713).

See also Beaconsfield, page 15; Chalfont St Giles, page 18.

Lacey Green
Grim's Ditch, page 55; **Lacey Green Windmill**, page 89; **Home of Rest for Horses**, page 92.

Lathbury
Church of All Saints, page 64.

Latimer
The chief interest in this pleasant village lies in the association with Lord Chesham, a statue of whom stands in the Market Square at Aylesbury. He lived at Latimer House and commanded the Imperial Yeomanry during the South African War. In the action at Boshof on 5th April 1900 a French colonel fighting for the Boers, the Comte de Villebois Mareuil, was killed. In a quixotic gesture, Chesham had the heart and ceremonial trappings of the Frenchman's horse buried on the village green at Latimer. The green also has a memorial to the men of the village killed in South Africa and paths of tiles taken from a Roman villa excavated in the nineteenth century.

Lavendon
Lavendon Castle, page 55.

The Lee
One of the county's curiosities is located on the bend of the road to the south of the village. A large figurehead of Admiral Lord Howe, taken from the Victorian warship of the same name, was set up here by the Liberty family in the 1920s, when the ship's timbers were purchased by them for the building of the family store in Regent Street, London. Howe's vic-

Jordans Meeting House.

Latimer village green and the grave of the Comte de Villebois Mareuil's horse.

tory at the naval engagement known as 'The Glorious First of June' is annually remembered at Penn Street while his superior at the battle, Admiral Lord Gambier, is recalled in the church at Iver.

Little Hampden
Church, page 64.

Little Horwood
Church of St Nicholas, page 65.

Little Kimble
Church of All Saints, page 65.

Little Missenden
Church of St John Baptist, page 65.

Long Crendon
Long Crendon was chosen in 1952 for filming in Coronation year as a typical English village. A centre of needlemaking in the nineteenth century, the village had been a wool centre in the middle ages, a relic of which is the Court House. The church is the setting for the annual Mystery Plays and the cottages along the High Street are picturesque.

Court House, page 74.

Lower Winchendon
See Nether Winchendon, page 36.

Maids Moreton
Church of St Edmund, page 65.

Marlow
Early closing Wednesday.
Marlow retains much of the character of the eighteenth century in the High Street, leading up from the suspension bridge and the Causeway to its junction at Market Place with West Street. The latter is also equally reminiscent of the eighteenth century. Market Place itself is overlooked by the former Town Hall, now the Crown, built by Samuel Wyatt in 1809. The obelisk in front is a milestone erected in 1822 on the so-called 'Gout Track', a turnpike route laid out for the Cecils of Hatfield House between their Hertfordshire mansion and the Bath Road at Reading.

West Street has a number of literary associations, Thomas Love Peacock having lived at Number 47 and Percy and Mary Shelley at Number 104, where Mary wrote *Frankenstein*. Remnantz in West Street was the first home of the Junior Division of the Royal Military College from 1802 until it moved to

Sandhurst in 1812. Off the High Street, Station Road has Marlow Place, a National Trust property not open to the public, which was built in 1720. Opposite Marlow Place, St Peter's Street may be followed to the site of the old Marlow bridge past the Old Parsonage and Deanery, parts of which date to the fourteenth century, Pugin's nineteenth-century Roman Catholic church, and the Two Brewers, in which Jerome K. Jerome wrote some of *Three Men in a Boat*. All Saints' Church is of interest while, at Little Marlow church, a few miles to the east, is the grave of Edgar Wallace.

Church of All Saints, page 65; **Roman Catholic Church of St Peter**, page 66; **Marlow Bridge**, page 89.

In the locality: Hog and Hollowhill Woods, page 48; Cliveden page 72; Dorney Court, page 72; Fawley Court, page 72. See also Bourne End, page 16; and Hambleden, page 28.

Medmenham
Hog and Hollowhill Woods, page 48.

Mentmore
Mentmore Towers, page 74.

Middle Claydon
Claydon House, page 71.

Milton Keynes
Market days in Central Milton Keynes, Tuesday and Saturday.

The name of the small village notable for its Decorated church has been given to the city designated in 1967 to accommodate a population of 250,000 by the end of the twentieth century. Incorporating three towns (Bletchley, Stony Stratford and Wolverton) and thirteen villages, the city of Milton Keynes covers 22,000 acres (8900 hectares). Although designed to take account of existing communities, the city has imposed a grid pattern of road communications on the area and 'Central Milton Keynes' has been located in the middle of the city area. Central Milton Keynes consists of a shopping concourse which is one of the largest covered centres in Europe with over 130 shops as well as a garden centre, restaurants, bars and public houses. However, it also has civic offices and a library, an 80 feet (24 metres) high mirror-glazed ziggurat containing the Point Entertainment Centre, the new Central Railway Station and a Central Business Centre,

Shelley's house at Marlow.

36 — *Towns and villages*

which, when completed, will be centred on the indoor landscaped terraces of the Winter Garden.

Commendably, many areas have been maintained as 'green lungs' with considerable attention to the provision of countryside recreational areas, a comprehensive 'Redway' system of paths for pedestrians and cyclists throughout the city area, as well as leisure centres at Stantonbury and Woughton. The city's rural and industrial past has been well preserved with archaeological finds displayed at Bradwell Abbey Discovery Centre, another museum at Stacey Hill, other archaeological sites at Bancroft, Loughton, Secklow and Woughton as well as various industrial relics. Some of the modern architecture is controversial, Liz Leyh's 'Concrete Cows' (at Bancroft off Monks Way) symbolising for many the character of much of the new city. However, there has been some imaginative use of the Grand Union Canal at Pennylands canalside housing development and the solar-powered housing at Great Linford is also of interest. Fifty energy-efficient homes are displayed at Energy World, which will form the basis of the Milton Keynes Energy Park. Future developments will include a scaled-down racing circuit for minicars at West Rooksley and a heliport at Kingston.

At Walton Hall, built in 1830, is the headquarters of the Open University, as revolutionary in its way as Buckingham's independent university.

Arc Wildfowl Centre, page 44; **Great Linford Manor House Park**, page 48; **Linford Wood**, page 49; **North Loughton Valley Park**, page 50; **Ouse Valley Park**, page 50; **Ouzel Valley Park**, page 50; **Mount Farm Lake**, page 49; **Stony Stratford Wildlife Conservation Area**, page 52; **Great Linford Brick Kilns**, page 89; **Willen Lakeside Park**, page 53; **Bancroft Roman Villa**, page 54; **Secklow Mound**, page 56; **Woughton Medieval Village**, page 56; **Church of All Saints**, page 66; **Church of Christ the Cornerstone**, page 66; **City Discovery Centre at Bradwell Abbey**, page 82; **Milton Keynes Exhibition Gallery**, page 83; **Milton Keynes Museum of In-**dustry and Rural Life, page 83; **Bradwell Tower Mill**, page 87; **Denbigh Hall Bridge**, page 87; **Iron Trunk Aqueduct**, page 89.

In the locality: Chicheley Hall, page 71; Cowper and Newton Museum, page 83; Weston Underwood Flamingo Gardens and Zoological Park, page 93. See also Bletchley, page 93; Newport Pagnell, page 36; Stony Stratford, page 39; Wolverton, page 42.

Moulsoe
Church of Assumption, page 66.

Mursley
Church of St Mary, page 66.

Nether Winchendon
Nether Winchendon House, page 74.

New Bradwell
Ouse Valley Park, page 50; Bradwell Tower Mill, page 87.

Newport Pagnell
Early closing Thursday.
The town has retained some of its character despite the development of industry, of which Tickford Bridge stands as a more elegant early representative. There is a tollhouse across the bridge and, opposite, the site of a twelfth-century abbey. Modern communications have bypassed the town but in former centuries it held an important position controlling the roads from London to the north. As such it was garrisoned by both sides in the Civil War. John Bunyan was briefly a member of the Parliamentary garrison and one of Oliver Cromwell's sons died of disease while serving here.
Tickford Bridge, page 90.
See also Milton Keynes, page 35.

North Crawley
Church of St Firmin, page 66.

Oakley
Shabbington Wood, page 51.

Olney
Early closing Wednesday; market day Thursday.

Concrete cows, Milton Keynes.

This small town is best-known for its association with John Newton and William Cowper (see page 97). Cowper's home is now a museum and a prominent feature of the Market Place. The spired church is of interest, as is the eighteenth-century bridge over the Ouse. The Market Place and High Street together present one of the best- preserved eighteenth-century townscapes in Buckinghamshire. There are some interesting Baptist associations with the 1893 chapel on the west side of the Market Place, surrounded by a graveyard that dates back to the seventeenth century. Number 23 in the High Street was once a seminary for Baptist missionaries established by John Sutcliff in 1799. Also in the High Street is a lace factory built in 1909, when efforts were being made to revive this once important rural industry. Olney is also well-known for the annual Pancake Race (see page 99).

Church of St Peter and St Paul, page 67; **Cowper and Newton Museum**, page 83; **Olney Bridge**, page 89.

In the locality: Emberton Park, page 47; Weston Underwood Flamingo Gardens and Zoological Park, page 93. See Newport Pagnell, page 36.

Penn

Located on a commanding spur of the Chilterns, Penn tends to be associated with William Penn (see page 95) but no direct connection has been established with the branch of the family that took its name from the village. Apart from the church of Holy Trinity, there are some noteworthy seventeenth-century almshouses while French School Meadow commemorates the establishment there in 1796 by Edmund Burke of a school for the sons or nephews of French aristocrats executed during the Revolution.

Church of Holy Trinity, page 67.

Pitstone

College Lake Wildlife Centre, page 46; Pitstone Hill, page 50; Pitstone Flint Mines, page 56; Church of St Mary, page 67; Pitstone Green Farm Museum, page 83; Pitstone Windmill, page 90; Grebe Canal Cruises, page 92.
See also Ivinghoe, page 31.

Prestwood

Prestwood Local Nature Reserve, page 50.

Princes Risborough

Early closing Wednesday.
Overlooked by Whiteleaf Cross, the town used to have the remains of a motte and bailey castle south-west of the church and took its royal title from the Black Prince, who repu-

tedly held a hunting lodge in the area. The town was granted the right to hold weekly markets, two annual fairs and two additional fairs in the reign of Henry VIII. To the east of the church is the Manor House, while Church Street leads into the Market Square with its Market Hall of 1824. Outside the library on the junction of Bell Street and the High Street is a memorial plaque erected in 1992 to Lieutenant Clyde Cosper of the USAAF, who stayed with his crippled Flying Fortress in order to ensure it did not crash on to the town in 1943. In neighbouring **Monks Risborough**, near St Dunstan's church, is a sixteenth-century stone dovecote.

Whiteleaf Hill, page 53; **Whiteleaf Cross**, page 56; **Princes Risborough Manor House**, page 75.

In the locality: Grangelands and Pulpit Hill Nature Reserve, page 48; Bledlow church, page 58; Bradenham church, page 58; Ellesborough church, page 61; Little Kimble church, page 65; Lacey Green Windmill, page 89; Home of Rest for Horses, page 92.

Quainton

The centre of the village is the Green domi-nated by the windmill but also containing the base and shaft of a fifteenth-century market cross, one of the few to survive even to this extent. Between the cross and the windmill, Cross Farmhouse dates from 1723 while Magpies Cottage was the home of the antiquarian George Lipscomb (1773-1846), whose *History of Buckinghamshire* was published in 1847. To the east of the Green is the church with its magnificent memorials, approached past the Old Rectory, with an eighteenth-century front, and the Winwood Almshouses erected in 1687. The road to Waddesdon leads to the Buckinghamshire Railway Centre at the former Quainton Road station.

Church of St Mary and Holy Cross, page 67; **Buckinghamshire Railway Centre**, page 87; **Quainton Windmill**, page 90.

In the locality: Waddesdon Manor, page 78; Wotton House, page 78.

Quarrendon

Quarrendon earthworks, page 56.

Radnage

Bottom Wood, page 44.

Monks Risborough dovecote

Ravenstone
Church of All Saints, page 67.

Saunderton
Lodge Hill, page 56.

Sherington
Church of St Laud, page 67.

Soulbury
Church of All Saints, page 67.

Steeple Claydon
An echo of the Civil War is to be found at Camp Barn in the main street opposite the road to Buckingham. A plaque of 1857 records that the barn provided the head-quarters for Oliver Cromwell, whose army was encamped around the site in March 1644 before the assault on the Royalist garrison at Hillesden House. Also to be noted is the Village Hall and Library, parts of which date back to the school founded by Sir Thomas Chaloner in 1656. Books for the library were later purchased with money given by Florence Nightingale, the sister-in-law of Sir Harry Verney of Claydon House, and her cheque is displayed inside the library.

In the locality: Claydon House, page 71.

Stewkley
Centenary Walk, page 45; Church of St Michael, page 68.

Stoke Mandeville
Bucks Goat Centre, page 91.

Stoke Poges
The village will always be associated with Thomas Gray, who lies buried in the church-yard of St Giles. Gray's home was West End House, now incorporated into Stoke Court. Near the church is a further monument to Gray (SU 977828), now in the care of the National Trust, which was erected by John Penn of Stoke Park in 1799. Both the monument and Stoke Park are the work of James Wyatt. The grounds of Stoke Park, upon which both 'Capability' Brown and Humphry Repton worked, also contain a monument to Sir Edward Coke, the Elizabethan lawyer who once owned the sixteenth-century Manor House. To the south of the church lie 30 acres (12 hectares) of the Memorial Gardens, open to the public during the week.

Church of St Giles, page 68.

In the locality: Burnham Beeches, page 45; Black Park, page 44; Langley Park, page 49; Rowley Farm Trail, page 51. See also Iver, page 31.

Stony Stratford
Market day Saturday.

Now part of the city of Milton Keynes, Stony Stratford retains many eighteenth-century buildings in the High Street and Church Street, most of which date from reconstruction after fires in both 1736 and 1742. Indeed, Sundial House at Number 40 Church Street has an inscription on its wooden sundial bearing the legend *Tempus et ignis omnis dunt* ('Time and fire destroy all things'). In the High Street, the Cock and Bull inns, allegedly the source of the saying, bear testimony to the past importance of the town as a staging post on Watling Street. There was once an Eleanor Cross, destroyed in the eighteenth-century conflagrations, and it was at Stony Stratford that the future King Richard III met the boy King Edward V, before accompanying him to London and the Tower. In the new shopping centre of Cofferidge Close an effort has been made to echo the era of inns and travellers by having each shop display its own hanging sign.

Ouse Valley Park, page 50; **Stony Stratford Wildlife Conservation Area**, page 52.

In the locality: Bancroft Roman Villa, page 54; City Discovery Centre at Bradwell Abbey, page 82. See also Bletchley, page 15; Milton Keynes, page 35; Wolverton, page 42.

Swanbourne
This small and pleasant village has associations with Nelson through the Fremantles. Captain Thomas (later Admiral) Fremantle was one of Nelson's 'Band of Brothers', his wife nursing Nelson after the loss of his arm at Santa Cruz. The Fremantle home, Swanbourne House, is now a preparatory school. The Manor House is Elizabethan while the Old House is sixteenth-century.

Taplow

Terrick

Thornborough

Tyringham

Like Gayhurst, there is no village as such at Tyringham but the house is of particular importance. Built for William Praed between 1792 and 1797, it was the work of Sir John Soane, although the interior was remodelled by G. F. Rees early in the twentieth century. At that time, too, the gardens were redesigned by Sir Edwin Lutyens but many of Soane's garden features were retained. Soane's original entrance gate in the form of an arch was described by Sir Nikolaus Pevsner as a 'monument of European importance' while Soane's bridge in the grounds is a listed monument.

Waddesdon

Sir John Soane's bridge at Tyringham.

Weedon

A delightful small village, Weedon has both seventeenth- and eighteenth-century buildings. Manor Farmhouse, for example, has datestones for 1649, 1674 and 1687 while both the Wheatsheaf and the Five Elms public houses have seventeenth-century features. Lilies, now an antiquarian booksellers with a number of interesting collections on display, was the home of Lord Nugent, author of a life of John Hampden. Many of the trees in the grounds of the house (the present structure dates from 1870) were planted by celebrities who visited Nugent, including Charles Dickens, Robert Browning and Lord John Russell (see page 95). Lilies is open to book buyers. Telephone: 01296 641393.

Wendover

Early closing Wednesday; market day Thursday.

A convenient centre for exploring the Chilterns and the Ridgeway, Wendover has some attractive buildings along the two main roads of Aylesbury Street and High Street. In the former, the frontage of Chiltern House dates from 1724 and the Red House is also eighteenth-century. In the High Street, past the Clock Tower of 1842 (now the tourist infor-

Cottages in Wendover.

mation office), Woolerton House is notable while, in the continuation of High Street known as Pound Street, Lime Tree House is mid-Georgian. A pocket borough until 1832, Wendover was represented by such distinguished parliamentarians as John Hampden and Edmund Burke, George Canning and Richard Steele. It was also the site of the first savings bank established in England in 1799. Robert Louis Stevenson stayed at the Red Lion on one occasion in 1875 and this inspired his essay *An Autumn Effect*.

Bacombe Hill, page 44; **Coombe Hill**, page 47; **Wendover Woods**, page 52.

In the locality: Boddington Camp Hillfort, page 54; Chequers, page 71; Chiltern Brewery, page 91. See also Princes Risborough, page 37.

Weston Turville
Weston Turville Reservoir, page 53.

Weston Underwood
Flamingo Gardens and Zoological Park, page 93.

West Wycombe
The village was saved from demolition in 1929 when it was bought by the National Trust. The buildings are mainly of the seventeenth and eighteenth centuries and include two old village inns. Also owned by the National Trust are West Wycombe Park, the grounds of which contain a lake, temples and statuary, and West Wycombe Hill. On the hill is St Lawrence's church, with a golden ball on top of its tower, and Sir Francis Dashwood's Mausoleum. The nearby caves provided the foundations for the road (now A40) linking the village to High Wycombe.

Church of St Lawrence, page 68; **West Wycombe Park**, page 78; **West Wycombe Caves and Mausoleum**, page 93.

Wexham
Rowley Farm Trail, page 51.

Whaddon
Lying at the heart of the once forested Whaddon Chase, the church is of interest. Whaddon Hall was the eighteenth-century

home of Browne Willis, who believed that Edmund Spenser wrote much of *The Faerie Queen* under an oak tree in the grounds in 1580. The present mansion, however, dates from 1820.
Church of St Mary, page 68.

Whitchurch

Retaining some impressive earthworks of Bolebec Castle and with a large church, Whitchurch enjoys fine views over the Vale of Aylesbury. The site of the former market cross is still apparent in the open area of Market Hill lying between the High Street and Oving Road. In Oving Road, Whitchurch House with its cartouche of two cherubs dates from the seventeenth century while the timber-framed old schoolhouse has sixteenth-century features. It was from the gardens of Bolebec House in Oving Road that Rex Whistler painted the Vale. In the High Street, the Priory Hotel dates from the fifteenth century. George Lipscomb once lived at Sycamores (see Quainton, above) while Jan Struther, author of *Mrs Miniver*, also lived in the village. Along the road to Winslow lie Creslow Manor, parts of which date from the fourteenth century, and a detached chapel dating from the twelfth century. Creslow Great Ground was once supposedly the largest open pasture field in England.
Bolebec Castle, page 54; **Church of St John Evangelist**, page 68.

Whiteleaf
Whiteleaf Hill, page 53; Whiteleaf Cross, page 56.

Willen
Willen Lakeside Park, page 53; Church of St Mary Magdalene, page 69.

Wing
Church of All Saints, page 69; Ascott House, page 70.

Winslow
Early closing Thursday; market days Monday and Tuesday.
The two most notable buildings in this small market town are the Baptist chapel and Winslow Hall. The Market Square itself has some pleasant eighteenth-century buildings and is the scene of the traditional Boxing Day meet of the Whaddon Chase Hunt.
Keach's Meeting House, page 69; **Winslow Hall**, page 78.
In the locality: Claydon House, page 71. See also Buckingham, page 18.

Wolverton
Market day Friday.
Now part of the city of Milton Keynes, Wolverton is primarily of interest to the industrial archaeologist with its railway architecture, embankment and canal aqueduct. Something of the rural past that predated the railway's arrival in the mid nineteenth century is recalled at the Museum of Industry and Rural Life.
Iron Trunk Aqueduct, page 89; **Milton Keynes Museum of Industry and Rural Life**, page 83.
In the locality: Bancroft Roman Villa, page 54; City Discovery Centre at Bradwell Abbey, page 82; Ouse Valley Park, page 50. See also Bletchley, page 15; Milton Keynes, page 35; and Stony Stratford, page 39.

Wooburn Common
Odds Farm Park Rare Breeds Centre, page 92.

Wooburn Green
Glass Craft, page 92.

Wotton Underwood
Wotton House, page 78; Church of All Saints, page 69.

3
The Buckinghamshire countryside

A feature of the early Buckinghamshire landscape was the large area covered by such forests as Whittlewood and Salcey in the north, Windsor in the south, Whaddon Chase in the east and the royal forest of Bernwood in the west. Most traces of these have long since disappeared but the county remains well wooded, notably in the Chilterns and the magnificent Burnham Beeches. Much of this woodland is relatively modern in terms of the development of the landscape and, although now automatically linked with Buckinghamshire, the beech has become the dominant tree only comparatively recently. Whatever their origins, however, areas such as Burnham Beeches, Bradenham Woods and Wendover Woods are resources of great importance while the Chilterns as a whole were designated an Area of Outstanding Natural Beauty in 1965. Elsewhere, nature trails and nature reserves have been laid out even in urban areas or in the quasi-industrial settings of gravel pits and canal banks.

Many areas of the county are good walking country, notably the Chilterns and the Thames valley. Footpath maps covering most of the Chilterns and prepared by the Chiltern Society are published by Shire Publications. Both the Chilterns and the Thames valley were areas of ancient settlement or communication and, in recent years, have become the focus for long-distance paths. Indeed, the County Council has promoted both linear and long-distance walks as well as bicycle and bridle routes. Leaflets produced for these paths are available from local libraries and tourist information offices (see page 101) but also from the Recreational Paths Officer, County Engineer's Department, Buckinghamshire County Council, County Hall, Aylesbury HP20 1UY. Telephone: 01296 382845.

Additional information on parks, walks and trails within Milton Keynes, for which another range of leaflets is available, can be obtained from Milton Keynes Parks Trust, 25 Erica Road, Stacey Bushes, Milton Keynes MK12 6LD. Telephone: 01908 223322. Similarly, information on the Forestry Commission's Chiltern Forest properties is available from the Chiltern Forest District Office, Upper Icknield Way, Aston Clinton, Aylesbury HP22 5NF. Telephone: 01296 625825. Wycombe District Council also promotes Wycombe Woodlands with a series of leaflets available from Wycombe Woodlands, Wycombe District Council, Leisure Department, Queen Victoria Road, High Wycombe HP11 1BB. Telephone: 01494 421827.

Some additional sites to those listed below maintained by the Berkshire, Buckinghamshire and Oxfordshire Naturalists Trust are open only to permit holders and enquiries should be directed to BBONT, Haydon Hill, Rabans Lane, Aylesbury HP19 3ST. Telephone: 01296 433222. Details of National Trust countryside properties may be obtained from the National Trust (Thames and Chiltern) Regional Office, Hughenden Manor, High Wycombe HP14 4LA. Telephone: 01494 528051.

Arc Wildfowl Centre, Great Linford, Milton Keynes (OS 152: SP 842428). Telephone: 01908 604810.

This wildfowl-breeding sanctuary run by the Game Conservancy is open only by prior appointment.

Aston Clinton Ragpits, Aston Clinton (OS 165: SP 888108). Off the road to St Leonards from A4011.

Many different herbs and shrubs and 27 species of butterfly can be found at this small site managed by BBONT among former chalk freestone or 'rag' pits.

Aylesbury Ring

One of the walks promoted by the County Council, the Aylesbury Ring consists of a 31 mile (50 km) circular walk divided into seven segments. Each segment varies between 2½ and 6 miles (5.5 and 10 km) and all lie within a 5 mile (8 km) radius of Aylesbury itself. A number of the County Council's suggested circular walks can also be reached from the route. It passes through Waddesdon, Hardwick, Weedon, Rowsham, Aston Clinton, Wendover, Great Kimble and Dinton.

Bacombe Hill, Wendover (OS 165: SP 864075). Just south-east of Wendover, off Ellesborough Road.

The Ridgeway National Trail crosses this area of open downland, scrub, hazel coppice and ash woodland. There are fine views over the Vale of Aylesbury.

Beeches Way

Another County Council suggested route, the Beeches Way comprises a 16 mile (26 km) trail across the south of the county from the Thames at Cookham in Berkshire to the Grand Union Canal at West Drayton in Middlesex. It passes through Burnham Beeches, Farnham Common, Fulmer, Black Park, Langley Park and Iver.

Black Park, Iver Heath (OS 176: TQ 010835). Telephone: 01753 511060. Car park in Black Park Road, signed off the A4007 between Uxbridge and Slough.

Black Park is a mixed woodland recreational area extending to 500 acres (202 hectares) with adjoining lake and self-guiding nature trails laid out by the County Council. There are not only walking paths but bridleways and even routes for horse-drawn carriages.

Bottom Wood, Radnage (OS 165: SU 793957). North of the A40 Stokenchurch to High Wycombe road, 5 miles (8 km) from High Wycombe.

A nature reserve owned by the Chiltern Society covers mostly ancient woodland. Over 150 species of plants are to be found including nine species of orchid. The wood is used by the

Black Park.

Chiltern Woodland Project as a demonstration site for woodland management. For information on the latter, contact: The Project Officer, Chiltern Woodlands Project, The Coppice, Winslow Gardens, High Wycombe HP13 7XY. Telephone: 01494 461286.

Bradenham Woods, Bradenham (OS 165: SU 823970). East of the A4010.

These woods are around the attractive village which, like the woods themselves, is mostly owned by the National Trust. The area features under the name of Hurstley in Disraeli's novel *Endymion*. The 30 acres (154 hectares) of the woods are typically Chiltern beech and whitebeam.

Brickhill Woods, Bow Brickhill (OS 152: SP 909335). Access from Little Brickhill or the car park on the road between Bow Brickhill and Woburn.

This is a mixed habitat of hardwood and conifer. On occasions, muntjac or 'barking deer', which escaped from Woburn Park, may be seen or heard. Blind Pond is a place associated with ghost stories over the years.

Buckingham Railway Walk, Buckingham (OS 152: SP 695334).

Wetland, woodland and calcareous grassland are the wildlife habitats that feature on this attractive walk along the route of a disused railway in Buckingham, near the town centre.

Burnham Beeches, Burnham (OS 175: SU 956852). West of the A355.

The area covers 574 acres (232 hectares) although this is only a remnant of a wooded area that once extended to Black Park, Iver Heath, Taplow and the Wooburn valley. Bought for public use by the Corporation of London in 1880, the beeches mostly date from the sixteenth century. The celebrated gnarled appearance of the trees has resulted from pollarding in former centuries – it ceased about 1820 – before wood was supplanted as a fuel in London by the seaborne coal trade. The woods have been visited by many celebrities, two of whom, the composer Mendelssohn and the singer Jenny Lind, are commemorated in landmarks. The beeches are a spectacular site

in autumn. For further information, contact the Head Keeper, Burnham Beeches Office, Hawthorn Lane, Farnham Common, Bucks SL1 3TB. Telephone: 01753 647358.

Canal Nature Reserve, Hyde Lane, Buckingham (OS 152: SP 726354).

This nature reserve comprises wetland habitat alongside the former branch of the Grand Junction Canal. It is managed by BBONT.

Captains Wood, Chesham (OS 165: SP 954034).

Footpaths and a bridleway cross this area of 27 acres (11 hectares) of beechwood on the edge of the town.

Centenary Walk, Kingsbridge, Stewkley (OS 165: SP 844237)

Starting at the Kingsbridge picnic site, this walk over County Council owned farmland follows Littlecote Brook and passes Centenary Plantation and Cublington Spinney, the latter planted to commemorate the local victory over the siting of London's third airport. For further information contact North Buckinghamshire Countryside Project Officer, Valuation and Estates Department, County Hall, Aylesbury HP20 1YH. Telephone: 01296 383392.

Chairborough Nature Reserve, Chairborough Road, Cressex, High Wycombe (OS 175: SU 848924).

Designated as a Local Nature Reserve in 1992 and once part of Hill Farm, this is an area of scrubland and woodland at which over 170 species of plant, twenty-three species of butterfly and thirty species of bird have been recorded. There is a short walk signed and laid out.

Chesham Bois Woods, Chesham Bois (OS 165: SP 960003).

This beech woodland habitat is managed by the Woodland Trust.

Chess Valley Walk

Jointly developed by Buckinghamshire County Council and the West Hertfordshire

View from Coombe Hill.

Countryside Management Project, this is a 10 mile (16 km) walk along the river Chess from Chesham to the Grand Union Canal at Rickmansworth.

Chiltern Link

This is an 8 mile (13 km) route promoted by the County Council from Wendover to Chesham, linking the Ridgeway with the Chess Valley Walk.

Church Farm Trail, Haddenham (OS 165: SP 744080).

This 1 mile (1.6 km) long trail around Church Farm views all kinds of wildlife in a working farm environment. The trail starts at the Stanbridge picnic site. For further information contact North Buckinghamshire Countryside Project Officer, Valuation and Estates Department, County Hall, Aylesbury HP20 1YH. Telephone: 01296 383392.

Church Wood Nature Reserve, Hedgerley (OS 175: SU 973873).

This 34 acre (14 hectare) site in mixed oak and beech woodland is managed by the Royal Society for the Protection of Birds. Over two hundred plant species have been recorded and over eighty species of bird.

College Lake Wildlife Centre, near Tring (OS 165: SP 935139). Off B488 between Ivinghoe and Tring.

This worked-out chalk quarry covers 100 acres (40 hectares) including a 25 acre (10 hectare) lake. It has been developed by BBONT in conjunction with Castle Cement since 1985 and has an information centre, bird observation hides and an arable weed research programme. There is a rich fauna of birds and butterflies, as well as plant life in a range of habitats. The centre is open daily to permit holders. Permits are available on site.

Colne Valley Park

Extending for 14 miles (22.5 km) and covering 40 square miles (104 square km) from Rickmansworth in Hertfordshire to Staines in Surrey, this regional park incorporates a number of other parks in Buckinghamshire including Black Park, Langley Park and Denham Country Park. Indeed, the Colne Valley Park Centre is situated at the last and presents interpretative displays including 'hands on' activities for children together with a full programme of talks and guided walks throughout the year. Open daily, the Centre also has refreshment facilities and offers full information on recreational opportunities in the park area as a whole. For more information, contact the Colne Valley Park Centre, Denham Country Park, Denham Court Drive, Denham UB9 5PG. Telephone: 01895 832662.

Coombe Hill, Wendover (OS 165: SP 849066). National Trust. Off Dunsmore Road, which is itself off the Ellesborough to Great Missenden road (car park at SP 852063).

Coombe Hill is the highest viewpoint in the Chilterns at 852 feet (260 metres), although the Chiltern summit in Wendover Woods is higher. At the top is a memorial to the men of Buckinghamshire who fell in the South African War. It was erected in 1904 and has been damaged by lightning on a number of occasions. There are spectacular views over the Vale of Aylesbury and the Chequers estate. Adjoining Coombe Hill is another National Trust property, Low Scrubs, an area of beech coppice.

Coombs Quarry, near Buckingham (OS 152: SP 733323). Reached by footpath from Thornborough Bridge (see page 90).

This site, of interest to geologists, is a disused limestone quarry with limekilns which may date back to Roman times.

Cross Bucks Way

This 24 mile (39 km) walk crosses the county from the Grand Union Canal near Linslade on the Bedfordshire boundary to the Oxfordshire border near Marsh Gibbon, passing through Soulbury, Stewkley, Swanbourne (linking with the Swans Way), Winslow, Addington (linking with the North Bucks Way), Hillesden, Twyford and Poundon. It also links with the Greensand Ridge Walk at the Bedfordshire end.

Denham Country Park, Denham Court Drive, Denham (OS 176: TQ 050865). Tele-

phone: 01895 835852. Signed from the A40/M40/A412/A4020 roundabout at junction 1 of the M40.

The park offers both woodland and meadowland habitats along the banks of the Colne and the Misbourne. Thus, a range of woodland and wetland invertebrates may be seen. The Grand Union Canal forms the eastern boundary of the park while both the Colne Valley Way and the South Bucks Way traverse it. It is the site of the Colne Valley Park Centre, opened in March 1992.

Emberton Park, Emberton, near Olney (OS 152: SP 882505). Off the A509.

Emberton Park is a 170 acre (68 hectare) recreational site on restored gravel pits with four lakes and a mile frontage along the river Ouse. A nature trail (SP 887502) has been laid out by BBONT.

Farnham Common Wood, Hedgerley (OS 175: SU 957867).

This small area of conifer woodland is crossed by paths, ideal for short strolls.

Gomm's Wood, Cock Lane, High Wycombe (OS 175: SU 895931).

Some 35 acres (14 hectares) of mixed habitat here range from beechwoods to chalk grassland and scrub under the management of the district council. It was chosen in 1992 as the first British Trust for Conservation (BTCV) demonstration wood in southern England. The intention is to foster community involvement in woodland conservation and management.

Gomm Valley, Gomm Road, High Wycombe (OS 175: SU 898922). North of the A40 between High Wycombe and Beaconsfield. Parking under the railway bridge close to the sawmill.

This BBONT site comprises chalk grassland and scrub rich in butterflies, moths and birds.

Grand Union Canal – Aylesbury Arm Walk

British Waterways and Aylesbury Countryside Management Project have laid out a 6

Grangelands and Pulpit Hill Nature Reserve.

mile (10 km) canalside walk from the Aylesbury canal basin to Marsworth junction.

Grangelands and Pulpit Hill Nature Reserve, Great Kimble (OS 165: SP 828048). East of the A4010 (car park for Pulpit Hill at SP 834045).

Grangelands is an area of chalk downland and woodland managed by BBONT. Pulpit Hill, which is owned by the National Trust, has beechwoods and is also the site (SP 832050) of a univallate iron age hillfort covering some 4 acres (1.6 hectares).

Great Linford Manor House Park, Great Linford, Milton Keynes (OS 152: SP 852422).

A nature trail has been laid out in the grounds of the early Georgian manor house and around the adjacent canal, disused railway and quarries. The almshouses and thatched barn of the former Linford estate have been converted into the Courtyard Art Centre by the Arts Workshop Trust, offering courses and performances. The Grand Union Canal is accessible through much of Milton Keynes but Linford Wharf has a mile long circular walk featuring information panels on the history of the former Newport Pagnell Canal, which joined the Grand Union at this point. The Great Linford Brick Kilns (see page 89) are also in the park.

Green Park, Stablebridge Road, Aston Clinton (OS 165: SP 887115). Telephone: 01296 630239.

A nature trail has been laid out by the county council in the grounds of the old manor house.

Hodgemoor Wood, Chalfont St Giles (OS 175: SU 968938). East of the A355.

Three nature trails have been laid out by the Forestry Commission in oak, beech and birch woods once used primarily for charcoal production and a beech and oak medieval coppice. There are also grassed picnic areas.

Hog and Hollowhill Woods, Medmenham (OS 175: SU 823860).

There is access by footpaths to these 80 acres (32.5 hectares) of mature former beech coppice, designated a Site of Special Scientific Interest.

Keephill Wood, Rye Dyke, High Wycombe (OS 175: SU 875925).

A mile-long (1.6 km) nature trail has been laid out along a beechwood hanger by Wycombe District Council and BBONT.

Originally common land for grazing, the site gradually changed to woodland after the turn of the twentieth century.

Kingcup Farm Trail, Denham (OS 176: SU 035851). On Willets Lane, off the A412. Telephone: 01753 511060.

Owned by the county council and farmed by tenants, the farm covers some 95 acres (38 hectares) and is given over primarily to growing fruit and vegetables. However, a 1½ mile (2.4 km) trail by the river Alderbourne features marsh marigolds or kingcups from April to June and the meadow and woodland habitat is open all year round.

Langley Park, Billet Lane, Iver Heath (OS 175: TQ 010817). Car park in Billet Lane, signed from the A4007 Uxbridge to Slough road.

Langley Park is a recreational area with a woodland setting, rhododendron gardens, and two nature trails laid out by the county council. Giant redwoods are featured in the park's 130 acres (52 hectares). There are views towards Windsor Castle.

Linford Wood, Linford, Milton Keynes (OS 152: SP 847403). Off H3 Monksway.

An area has been set aside for wildlife conservation while the 100 acre (40 hectare) site also includes bridlepaths, a jogging circuit and keep-fit trail.

Mount Farm Lake, Bond Avenue, Bletchley (OS 152: SP 871350).

This is a circular walk around disused gravel pits which now support a variety of wildfowl. Lakeside facilities include a public house, pitch and putt course, tennis courts and children's play area.

North Bucks Way

Designated by the Ramblers Association in 1972, the North Bucks Way comprises 30 miles (48 km) of footpath branching off the Ridgeway at Chequers Knap and linking with the Grafton Way on the Northamptonshire boundary at Wolverton. It passes through Great Kimble, Hartwell, Waddesdon, Quainton, East Claydon, Addington, Great Horwood, Nash and Whaddon. A guide is available from the Ramblers Association, 1-5 Wandsworth Road, London SW8 2XX. However, it is also sold at many points in the county itself and the county council has also produced a leaflet as part of their series on linear and long-distance walks.

A pathway through Linford Wood.

North Loughton Valley Park, Milton Keynes (OS 152: SP 831388).

Effectively a corridor along Loughton Brook from New Bradwell to Loughton including old grassland areas managed as wildflower meadows, this includes the reconstructed Bancroft Roman Villa (see page 54).

Northmoor Hill Wood, Denham (OS 176: TQ 034888). Off Tilehouse Lane, Denham. Telephone: 01753 511060.

A woodland trail has been laid out by the county council and the British Trust for Conservation Volunteers.

Ouse Valley Park, Milton Keynes (OS 152: SP 801414).

A riverside walk follows the Ouse between Stony Stratford and New Bradwell and, while it is crossed by the A5, the Grand Union Canal and the main-line railway, it still provides a varied recreational area. The Iron Trunk (see page 89) may be viewed from the park as well as the site of Wolverton's medieval village and there is a public hide for birdwatching overlooking the Stony Stratford Wildlife Conservation Area.

Ouzel Valley Park, Milton Keynes (OS 152: SP 880395 to 881361).

This runs through the eastern part of the city between Willen Lake and Caldecotte Lake and close to Simpson, Woolstone and Woughton-on-the-Green. Information panels have been established for sites of historic interest around Woolstone.

Pavis Woods, near Tring (OS 165: SP 905086 and 915092).

Crossed by the Ridgeway National Trail and other paths and bridleways, these 87 acres (35 hectares) of ancient woodland include ash and oak woodland, coppice and beech high forest.

Picnic sites

The County Council's Countryside Management Service provides a number of picnic sites in rural locations. They all have car parks and access to local footpaths. The sites, with grid references, are:

Ashgrove, Little Missenden (OS 165: SP 935987).

Black Park, Wexham (see page 44).

Caps Wood, Tatling End (OS 176: TQ 020872).

Cockshoots Wood, near Wendover (OS 165: SP 872042).

Holtspur, Wooburn Green (OS 175: SP 921893).

Kingsbridge, near Stewkley (OS 165: SP 844237).

Northmoor Hill Wood, near Denham (OS 176: TQ 035891).

Pitstone Hill, near Ivinghoe (see below).

Prestwood Local Nature Reserve, near Prestwood (see below).

Shipton Bridge, near Winslow (OS 165: SP 777269).

Spade Oak, Little Marlow (OS 175: SU 884873).

Stanbridge, Haddenham (OS 165: SP 746081).

Thornborough Bridge, near Buckingham (see page 90).

Thorney Country Park, Iver (see page 52).

Three Locks, near Soulbury (OS 165: SP 893282).

Whielden Gate, near Amersham (OS 165: SP 938956).

Whiteleaf Hill, near Princes Risborough (see page 53).

Pitstone Hill, near Ivinghoe (OS 165: SP 955149).

Designated a Site of Special Scientific Interest, 54 acres (22 hectares) of open downland here are crossed by the Ridgeway National Trail and other paths.

Prestwood Local Nature Reserve, Prestwood (OS 165: SP 867992).

There is a small area of downland and scrub, with picnic facilities, owned by Wycombe District Council. It is a good place to see butterflies in summer.

Ridgeway National Trail

Opened as a long-distance National Trail by the Countryside Commission in 1972, the 90 miles (145 km) of the Ridgeway from Avebury in Wiltshire to Ivinghoe Beacon in Buckinghamshire are part of the central sec-

Caps Wood picnic site.

tion of a far longer prehistoric route stretching from the Dorset coast to the Wash. In Buckinghamshire (OS 165: SP 770013 to SP 961168) the path follows the course of the Upper Icknield Way along the chalk scarp of the Chilterns from near Bledlow to Ivinghoe. Many of the county's ancient monuments overlook the course of the Ridgeway, which also embraces parts of the Chequers estate, Pulpit Hill and Coombe Hill. Most sections are readily accessible, and Countryside Commission guides are available at most tourist information centres. An information and accommodation guide is available from the Ridgeway Officer, Countryside Service, Department of Leisure and Arts, Oxfordshire County Council, Holton, Oxford OX33 1QQ. Telephone: 01865 810224.

Rowley Farm Trail, Black Park Road, Wexham, near Slough (OS 176: TQ 005828). For information telephone the South Buckinghamshire Countryside Project Officer: 01753 511060. Park at the Black Park car park (see page 44).

Rowley Farm belongs to Buckinghamshire County Council, which has waymarked a 2½ mile (4 km) trail around the farmland and the adjoining Rowley Woods, a mixed woodland with areas of coppice, alder and conifers. The trail visits arable fields as well as permanent pasture grazed by the dairy herd and enables visitors to learn about the wildlife and agriculture of the countryside adjoining Black Park.

Rushbeds Wood, near Brill (OS 165: SP 668157).

This BBONT woodland site of 106 acres (43 hectares) is open to the public along its rides. Almost two hundred species of plant have been recorded and muntjac, fallow deer and fox are present.

Shabbington Wood, Oakley (OS 165: SP 615115).

Part of the Forestry Commission's Chiltern Forest District and designated as a Site of Special Scientific Interest, the wood is planted with Norway spruce and oak and offers two nature trails. One, the Bernwood Butterfly Trail, enables visitors to spot some of the forty species recorded in the wood. A special leaflet for the trail is available on site.

South Bucks Way

This 23 mile (37 km) route links the Ridgeway at Coombe Hill with the Grand

Union Canal at Denham, passing through Little Hampden, Great Missenden, Little Kingshill, Little Missenden, Amersham, Chalfont St Giles and Chalfont St Peter and following the valley of the Misbourne for much of the way.

Stockgrove Country Park, near Great Brickhill (OS 165: SP 919294).

Jointly managed by Buckinghamshire and Bedfordshire County Councils, Stockgrove's 80 acres (32 hectares) comprise ancient woodland, parkland and a lake. There is a visitor centre and the activities that are available include walking, orienteering and birdwatching.

Stony Stratford Wildlife Conservation Area, Stony Stratford (OS 152: SP 788410). Off the A5. Telephone: 01908 313704.

A riverside meadow in old gravel workings is managed by BBONT with some areas open only to BBONT members, although there is a public hide in the Ouse Valley Park. Waders and other wildfowl can be seen.

Swans Way

This is essentially a long-distance bridle-path rather than a walking route and covers a total distance of 65 miles (105 km) from Goring in Oxfordshire to the Salcey Forest on the Northamptonshire border. It enters Buckinghamshire near Bledlow and passes through Ilmer, Stone, North Marston, Swanbourne, Whaddon and Milton Keynes.

Thame Valley Walk

A joint venture of Aylesbury Countryside Management Project, the National Rivers Authority and the Ramblers Association, the walk starts at Haydon Mill on the north-western edge of Aylesbury, links with the North Bucks Way near Eythrope and joins the Oxfordshire Way at Albury, a distance of 15 miles (24 km). It passes through Nether Winchendon, Chearsley, Long Crendon and Shabbington. Characteristic features are pollarded willows and wetland habitats.

Thames Path and London Countryway

A footbridge recently opened at Temple on

the Thames near Marlow has effectively completed the Countryside Commission's long-distance path from Greenwich to the river's source near Kemble in Gloucestershire. Many stretches of the riverside in Buckinghamshire are accessible for walks or picnics, with boats for hire at a number of riverside locations. The footbridge over the weir at Hambleden is a particularly attractive place, while Boulter's Lock at Maidenhead, the pound locks of which were originally constructed in 1772, is popular with sightseers. The lock lies only 1^1/2 miles (2.4 km) downstream from Cliveden, from the grounds of which there are justifiably famous views of the river. Marlow lies on the river and the town is also on the London Countryway, a long-distance path encircling the capital, which passes on in a north-easterly course to West Wycombe, Great Missenden and Chesham before crossing the county boundary again. Information on the Thames Path may be obtained from the Thames Path Project Officer, c/o Thames Water Authority, Amenities and Recreation Department, Nugent House, Vastern Road, Reading, Berkshire RG1 9DB. Telephone: 01734 593530.

Thorney Country Park, Richings Park, Iver (OS 176: TQ 045788).

Part water and part landscaped grassland, the country park covers 50 acres (20 hectares) of former mineral workings beside the M25. There are picnic facilities, walks and opportunities for birdwatching.

Three Shires Way

A bridle route of 37 miles (60 km) runs from Tathall End near Hanslope north into Bedfordshire and Cambridgeshire.

Two Ridges Link

An 8 mile (13 km) route connects the Ridgeway at Ivinghoe Beacon, via Slapton, with the Greensand Ridge Walk at Linslade in Bedfordshire.

Wendover Woods, Wendover.

The Forestry Commission has laid out nature trails at Boddington Banks, Aston Hill, Beech Hangings and School Trail (OS 165:

Peace Pagoda, Milton Keynes.

SP 889090), Daniel's Trudge (SP 891101) and Hale View (SP 895082). Starting points for the trails are at the car park at Halton Wood picnic place off the road to St Leonards, for which there is no charge. A charge is made for taking vehicles further into the woods, which provide a habitat for the firecrest, and one of the trails is laid among the bird's favoured Norway spruces. In addition to the walking routes, there are a permanent orienteering course, a fitness trail, children's play area and footpaths to the iron age hillfort of Boddington Camp (see page 54).

Weston Turville Reservoir, Weston Turville (OS 165: SP 862096).

The reservoir was originally intended to supply water to the Grand Union Canal and the paths around it are open to the public under an agreement between BBONT and the British Waterways Board. Apart from breeding colonies of ducks, the reservoir also provides opportunities to view migrant and wintering waterfowl.

Whiteleaf Hill, near Princes Risborough (OS 165: SP 823036).

This is a fine viewpoint on the Chiltern escarpment, overlooking the Vale of Aylesbury. There are 27 acres (11 hectares) of woodland and grassland and features include the Whiteleaf Cross hill figure and prehistoric burial mounds (see page 56). There are picnic facilities near the car park. The Ridgeway National Trail passes through the area.

Willen Lakeside Park, Brickhill Street, Milton Keynes (OS 152: SP 878409). Off Childs Way and linking with the Ouzel Valley Park.

Willen has 170 acres (69 hectares) of recreational space in an urban setting. The north lake (OS 152: SP 879407) is a conservation area with interesting birdwatching. There is a nature trail and the lake is overlooked by a Japanese Buddhist 'peace pagoda', the first built in the western hemisphere. The south lake (SP 880400) is recreational, with lakeside development which includes an hotel, restaurant and water sports facilities.

4
Ancient monuments

Many traces remain of the impact of past generations upon the Buckinghamshire landscape. Amongst the earliest discernible of these are round barrows and ring-ditches associated with the bronze age. Of the iron age, there are not only a number of hillforts, most which are located along the Chiltern scarp, but also the linear earthworks known as Grim's Ditch. Roman remains are less readily identified, with the exception of the burial mounds at Thornborough. By far the most plentiful remains are of the Norman and later medieval period. At least eighteen castles were erected in Buckinghamshire by the Normans but all appear to have been of the motte and bailey type, with none subsequently reconstructed in stone. Over 150 moated sites have been recorded while there are also many other earthworks ranging from medieval fishponds and deer parks to at least a hundred deserted village sites. In common with other counties with chalk escarpments, there are figures cut in the chalk at Bledlow and Whiteleaf.

Many of the sites can be readily interpreted only by the specialist and guidance should be sought from the County Museum at Aylesbury or the Bradwell Abbey Discovery Centre. Therefore only those sites most easily identified and accessible are listed here.

Bancroft Roman Villa, Wolverton (OS 152: SP 840419).

Within Loughton Valley Park, reconstructed foundations of a fourth-century Roman villa are supplemented by information panels. A reconstructed mosaic pavement from the villa is displayed in Queen's Court in Central Milton Keynes.

Bledlow Cross, Bledlow (OS 165: SP 770009). On Wain Hill, south-west of Bledlow village.

Bledlow Cross, cut into the chalk on Wain Hill, measures some 75 feet (23 metres) transversely. It is of unknown origin but may have been cut as late as the seventeenth century. The hill itself is associated with other archaeological features, the Cop (SP 773012) on the northern slope being the remains of a round barrow which yielded part of a polished stone axe when excavated in the 1930s.

Boddington Camp Hillfort, Halton (OS 165: SP 882080). Accessible along forest paths south-east of Wendover.

The iron age hillfort on Boddington Hill covers some 17 acres (7 hectares) to the south-west of Halton Wood.

Bolebec Castle, Whitchurch (OS 165: SP 799207). Off a minor road west of the village centre.

Bolebec Castle has some well-preserved earthworks of a former motte and bailey. There is a tradition locally of the castle being rebuilt in stone and a few rocky outcrops survive on the summit of the motte.

Bulstrode Camp, Gerrards Cross (OS 175: SU 994880). West of the B416 Gerrards Cross to Slough road.

The 22 acre (9 hectare) hillfort surrounded by double ditches and ramparts is the largest in Buckinghamshire. It is a public open space.

Castlethorpe Castle, Castlethorpe (OS 152: SP 798446). West of the village church.

Castlethorpe Castle comprises the remains of a motte and bailey structure, the motte now being some 36 feet (11 metres) high. It lies to the west of the church, which is itself surrounded by ditches up to 60 feet (18 metres) wide. A particularly large structure with both inner and outer baileys, the castle was destroyed in 1215.

Cholesbury Camp, Cholesbury (OS 165: SP 930072). In the centre of the village.

Cholesbury Camp is an iron age fort whose excavation in 1932 revealed Belgic occupation in the first century BC. It is some 15 acres (6 hectares) in extent and encloses the church of St Lawrence rebuilt in 1872-3.

Grim's Ditch

The linear system of Grim's Ditch is to be found in many areas to the south of the crest of the Chiltern scarp. Long sections are those from Redland End to Hampden House (SP 834022 to 845026) and from Park Wood, Bradenham, to Grymsdyke House at Lacey Green (SU 828989 to 827996). Shorter sections are to be found elsewhere in Great and Little Hampden, Cholesbury, Great Missenden, St Leonards, Lacey Green and Pitstone. Consisting simply of a bank and ditch, the system is usually regarded as being iron age in origin. There have been conflicting theories as to its purpose but the most likely interpretation is that it marked an early

A nineteenth-century view of Whiteleaf Cross.

pastoral boundary, dividing pasture from lower-lying arable land.

Ivinghoe Beacon, Ivinghoe (OS 165: SP 961169). West of Ivinghoe and immediately south of the B489 to Dunstable; there is a car park on the minor road to Ringshall. National Trust.

Ivinghoe Beacon is not the largest hillfort in the county – that distinction is held by Bulstrode Camp – but it is probably the most important as it is now believed to be one of the earliest in Britain. Abandoned in the eighth century BC, it covers over 5 acres (2 hectares) and has a single bank and ditch. The hill also marks the end of the Ridgeway Path and commands wide views over the surrounding country. A round barrow on the summit is of bronze age origin.

Lavendon Castle, Lavendon (OS 152: SP 917544). North of the village church.

Lavendon Castle comprises extensive earthworks to the north of the church, suggesting that the Norman motte was surrounded by no less than three baileys. The motte was levelled in the 1940s.

Lodge Hill, Saunderton (OS 165: SU 795998). The hill is crossed by the Ridgeway Path running east from the minor road between Bledlow and Bledlow Ridge to the road between Saunderton and Saunderton Lee.

Lodge Hill has the remains of an iron age settlement, represented by a series of depressions in the ground, as well as two ploughed bell barrows.

Pitstone Flint Mines, Ivinghoe (OS 165: SP 950142). Car park 1 mile (1.6 km) south of Ivinghoe, along the minor road to Aldbury.

A small group of neolithic flint mines is sited on the western angle of Pitstone Hill. The iron age Grim's Ditch curves round them on the slope of the hill.

Quarrendon, Aylesbury (OS 165: SP 806156). To the north-west of Aylesbury.

East of the present Church Farm and the former church of St Peter, on the brow of the hill are earthworks of a gun battery that formed part of Aylesbury's defences during the Civil War, when the town was garrisoned for Parliament between 1642 and 1646. Remains of a deserted medieval village lie between here and the church and the site of the mansion of the Lee family, at which Queen Elizabeth I was entertained in August 1592. There is a second deserted medieval village between that and Church Farm.

Secklow Mound, Central Milton Keynes (OS 152: SP 862365). Situated behind Milton Keynes Library.

This is a reconstruction with accompanying information panels of the traditional meeting mound for the Secklow Hundred of the Anglo-Saxon period.

Thornborough Mounds, Thornborough (OS 165: SP 732332). On the north side of the A421 Buckingham to Bletchley road, 250 yards (229 metres) west of Thornborough Bridge.

Thornborough Mounds are two Roman burial mounds of the second century AD, excavated for the Duke of Buckingham and Chandos in 1839, when the finds were sent to the Cambridge University Museum of Archaeology and Anthropology.

Westend Hill and Southend Hill, Cheddington (OS 165: SP 919165). South-west of the village.

Visible on the slopes of Westend Hill and Southend Hill are the traces of lynchets. These were broad terraces produced by the constant ploughing of strips for cultivation parallel to the contours of the hill in ancient times. Aerial photography has revealed a ploughed-out iron age hillfort on Southend Hill.

Whelpley Hill Fort, Ashley Green (OS 165: SP 996040). North of the B4505 Chesham to Hemel Hempstead road.

At Whelpley Hill there is a poorly preserved iron age plateau fort with a single rampart, covering some 4½ acres (1.8 hectares).

Whiteleaf Cross, Whiteleaf (OS 165: SP 821039). Beside the minor road from Monks Risborough to Great Hampden; from a car park at the top of the hill the Ridgeway Path leads to the top of the cross.

Whiteleaf Cross, which was incorporated in the arms of the county in 1947, is of uncertain origin although the site was occupied by some kind of boundary mark in AD 903. However, the cross is possibly much later in date and conceivably the work of medieval monks from Monks Risborough or Missenden Abbey. In the nineteenth century the scouring of the 30 by 80 feet (9 by 24 metres) cross was an annual custom. Above the cross, Whiteleaf Fields (SP 814043) command a view over the Vale of Aylesbury. The Whiteleaf barrow, above the cross, is of neolithic date and was found to contain the body of a man in a wooden burial chamber when excavated between 1935 and 1939.

Woughton Medieval Village, Milton Keynes (OS 152: SP 871376). Within the Ouzel Valley Park at Woughton Green.

A trail with information panels has been established around the earthworks of the former medieval village of Woughton-on-the-Green, which was deserted around the seventeenth century.

5
Churches and chapels

Churches are the most substantial survivals of medieval architecture in the county. Few have any pre-Norman features, although there is a notable exception at Wing, and the majority date from the thirteenth century onwards. Stewkley and Fingest are particularly fine examples of the Norman style while most of the successive changes in church architecture are also well represented. Aylesbury and High Wycombe, for example, display Early English features (1180-1300). Emberton and Sherington are representative of the Decorated style (1300-50) and Hillesden and Maids Moreton of the Perpendicular style (1350-1550). Willen is a marvellous example of Georgian Baroque while the Gothic revival is evident at Hartwell and Fenny Stratford.

Whatever their origins, many Buckinghamshire churches display the often heavy hand of the Victorian restorers, notably the Oxford diocesan architect G. E. Street and George Gilbert Scott. Indeed, Scott (1811-78) was born at Gawcott, where his father was the curate, and was inspired originally by the architecture of nearby Hillesden. Earlier the local antiquarian Browne Willis (1682-1760) had also turned his hand to church restoration as at Bletchley and Fenny Stratford.

Towers are the most common external features of Buckinghamshire churches but two fine spires are to be found at Hanslope and Olney and Princes Risborough has an attractive steeple. Of internal features, the county's churches have many fine brasses, one of the earliest of which is at Pitstone. A fine range of fonts includes a local twelfth-century 'Aylesbury' style while a number have medieval tiles deriving from kilns at Penn and Tylers Green. Monuments include those in the celebrated Bedford Chapel at Chenies and there are fine wall paintings at such churches as Broughton, Chalfont St Giles, Little Hampden, Little Kimble and Little Missenden.

In medieval times there were some monastic foundations but few have survived: the largest remains are of Augustinian orders at Burnham Abbey and Notley Abbey (both parts of private residences not open to the public) and of the Benedictine foundation at Bradwell (see page 82). There are also some early examples of nonconformist architecture, especially at Jordans (see page 31) and Winslow. Later nineteenth-century churches include a Roman Catholic church at Marlow by A. W. N. Pugin.

Amersham: St Mary.

The chief interest in this church, restored by the Victorians, lies in the monuments to the Drake family of Shardeloes. In the Drake Chapel the monument to Montague Drake (died 1728) is by Scheemakers while an urn for William Drake (died 1802) is especially fine. The monument to Henry Curwen (died 1636) by Edward Marshall should also be noted. The seventeenth-century glass in the east window was brought from Lamer House in Hertfordshire in 1760.

The Friends' Meeting House in Whielden Street dates from 1689 and the Baptist Meeting House, behind the King's Arms in the High Street, from 1783.

Aylesbury: St Mary.

Over-restored by George Gilbert Scott between 1850 and 1869 and restored again in the late 1970s, the church retains an Early English west door and chancel, in which Scott

St Mary's church, Aylesbury.

replaced the fifteenth-century east window with three lancets. There is a lovely twelfth-century 'Aylesbury' font and a rare fifteenth-century vestment press is in the south transept. The alabaster monument to Lady Lee (died 1584) was brought from the disused church at Quarrendon.

Beaconsfield: St Mary and All Saints.

The church was completely restored in 1869 and its interest lies in the monuments. Edmund Burke has a brass tablet set in the floor beneath the front pews while he is also commemorated by a memorial on the south wall. The font was the gift of Edmund Waller, who lies buried in the churchyard under a conspicuous obelisk by William Stanton. Other families recalled are the Burnhams, Du Prés and Grenfells, one window remembering the Grenfell twins, Francis and Riversdale,

who fell in the First World War.

Bierton: St James. (On A418 north-east of Aylesbury.)

Most of the church is fourteenth-century with some Decorated doorways and windows and a plain Norman font. There are remains of wall paintings and a monument to H. P. Layard, father of the archaeologist who discovered Nineveh. The monument to Samuel Bosse (died 1616) depicts husband and wife kneeling with seven children and a further six children in cots.

Bledlow: Holy Trinity. (Off B4009 south-west of Princes Risborough.)

This twelfth-century building, widened in the thirteenth century, was again enlarged in the fourteenth century. There are an 'Aylesbury' font and an eighteenth-century reredos by John Gwynne, painted by Samuel Wale. The wall paintings include a fourteenth-century depiction of Adam and Eve over the south doorway and a later version of St Christopher on the north wall.

Bletchley: St Mary.

The church was restored by Browne Willis and again by William White in the nineteenth century. The chancel dates from the thirteenth century, the north aisle from the fourteenth century and the west tower is Perpendicular. Richard, Lord Grey de Wilton (died 1442), has an alabaster monument, while a skeleton digging a grave is engraved on a slab with a brass plate to Thomas Sparke (died 1616).

Bradenham: St Botolph. (Off A4010 between High Wycombe and Princes Risborough.)

The Norman south doorway is believed to be one of the earliest in the county. The eighteenth-century heraldic glass with the crest of Thomas, Lord Windsor, in the east window of the north chapel is a very early example of enamelled glass. Monuments include those of Charles West (died 1684) and Isaac D'Israeli (1766-1848).

Broughton: St Lawrence. (Off A5130 south of Newport Pagnell.)

Bledlow church.

Mostly fourteenth-century with a Perpendicular west tower, the church is best-known for its retouched fourteenth- and fifteenth-century wall paintings. These include St George and a Doom (or Last Judgement) featuring the Weighing of Souls and a Warning to Swearers. A pietà includes backgammon players.

Buckingham: St Peter and St Paul.

This church was built between 1777 and 1781 on the site of the former motte and bailey castle to replace an older church in decay. It was almost entirely remodelled by George Gilbert Scott after 1862 and a chancel was added for the third Duke of Buckingham and Chandos in 1882.

Burnham: St Peter. (North of A4 between Slough and Maidenhead.)

This is a mostly thirteenth-century church extended in the next two centuries. There are sixteenth-century brasses to the Eyre family which are palimpsests of earlier Flemish brasses. Monuments include those to John Wright (died 1594), George Evelyn (died 1657) and Mr Justice Willes (died 1787), while Lord Grenville (see page 94) is buried here. On the south arcade piers are anti-papal slogans, 'The Pope is a knave' and 'The Pope is a vilin', probably eighteenth-century.

Chalfont St Giles: St Giles. (Off A413 southeast of Amersham.)

Restored by Street but retaining a Perpendicular west tower, the church is most notable for retouched fourteenth-century wall paintings which illustrate the Life of the Virgin, part of the Creation, scenes of the Life of St John the Baptist and a Crucifixion. A later fifteenth-century wall painting is of an architectural design while there are brasses and monuments to the Fleetwood family. The showman Bertram Mills is buried in the churchyard.

Chearsley: St Nicholas. (North of Thame.)

Though mostly Perpendicular in style, the church has an earlier 'Aylesbury' font. A brass on the chancel floor to John Frankeleyn (died 1462) and his wife includes their seven children. The church has the royal arms of both George II and George III and retains a timbered west gallery of 1761-2.

Chenies: St Michael. (Off A404 between Amersham and Rickmansworth.)

Rebuilt in both the fifteenth and the nineteenth centuries, the church retains a Norman font and the fifteenth-century Cheyne brasses. However, the most celebrated feature is the mortuary chapel of the Russells. Although not open to the public, it may be viewed through a plate-glass division. Regarded as the richest collection of family monuments in any English church, it reflects the association of the Russell family, later Earls and Dukes of Bedford, with the parish from the fifteenth to the eighteenth century, when the family seat moved to Woburn Abbey but Russells continued to be buried here. The earliest monument is to John Russell, first Earl of Bedford (died 1555) and by far the largest is to the fifth Earl and first Duke (died 1700). Lord John Russell (see page 95) is also buried in the chapel. The village also has a Baptist chapel of 1778.

Chetwode: St Mary and St Nicholas. (Off A421 south-west of Buckingham.)

Formerly the chancel of an Augustinian priory, founded in 1245, this became a parish church after dissolution in 1480. There are some fine Early English windows and some of the best early glass in the county, dating from the thirteenth and fourteenth centuries and depicting figures and coats of arms.

Chilton: St Mary. (Off B4011 between Thame and Bicester.)

The interesting appearance derives from fifteenth-century restructuring, which left the chancel lop-sided, and from the lower north tower. There are both Early English and Perpendicular features, an eighteenth-century organ from Chilton House and monuments to the Croke family. There is also a monument to Chief Justice Carter (died 1755), who had Chilton House rebuilt after 1740. The First World War battlefield cross should also be noted.

Clifton Reynes: St Mary. (Just east of Olney.)

The church is in the Perpendicular style with a fourteenth-century font depicting the Virgin, Trinity and saints. A main interest is the Reynes Chapel. Two pairs of knights and ladies of about 1300 are the only wooden effigies in the county but, like a later fourteenth-century stone monument, the identity of the subjects is unknown. There is a brass to Sir John Reynes (died 1428) and a bust by Scheemakers to Alexander Small (died 1752).

Cuddington: St Nicholas. (Off A418 south-west of Aylesbury.)

Something of a local landmark, the church has a complicated architectural history, with the original twelfth-century building being altered no less than four times during the thirteenth century alone before final restoration by G. E. Street in 1857. There is a First World War battlefield cross and, on the outside wall, an interesting tablet to the forty-eight victims of a cholera epidemic in the nearby hamlet of Gibraltar in 1849.

Denham: St Mary. (Off A40 north-west of Uxbridge.)

The main interest in this largely Perpendicular church lies in the interior features. The thirteenth-century font is of Purbeck marble while there is a remnant of a fifteenth-century Doom over the south doorway. Sir Edmund Peckham (died 1564) has a tomb chest and there are some good brasses including that of Agnes Jordan (died 1544), the last abbess of Syon at Brentford, which is one of only two extant brasses to an abbess in England.

Dinton: St Peter and St Paul. (Off A418 south-west of Aylesbury.)

The Norman south doorway, with its elaborately sculptured tympanum of wyverns consuming fruit from the Tree of Life and St Michael fighting a dragon on the lintel, is a remarkable piece of work. There is a Jacobean pulpit and an altar table of 1606, eighteenth-century communion rails and a number of brasses, including one to Simon Mayne (died 1617).

Drayton Beauchamp: St Mary. (Off A41 west of Tring.)

St Mary's church, Edlesborough.

This is a decorated structure with Perpendicular windows, of which the restored east window is notable for depicting ten of the twelve apostles. A large monument commemorates William Cheyne, Viscount Newhaven (died 1728). In the chancel are fine brasses to two knights Thomas Cheyne (1368) and William Cheyne (1375). The author and divine Richard Hooker (1553-1600) was rector before becoming Master of the Temple in 1585.

Edlesborough: St Mary. (On A4146 southeast of Leighton Buzzard.)

A landmark on its small hill amid the lower-lying Vale of Aylesbury, the church had a spire until it was destroyed by lightning in 1828. The west tower is Decorated but much of the remainder is Perpendicular, including the fifteenth-century canopied pulpit and the rood screen. Brasses include that of John de Swynstede (died 1395) and an unusual rose design of John Killingworth (died 1412), which was brought from the chapel at Ashridge House.

Ellesborough: St Peter and St Paul. (Just west of Wendover.)

Not unlike Edlesborough in its prominent position, the church was restored between 1854 and 1871. The principal interest is the monument to Bridget Croke (died 1638), the daughter and heiress of William Hawtrey of Chequers.

Emberton: All Saints. (On A509 south of Olney.)

The west tower is Perpendicular but the remainder represents one of the best examples of the Decorated style in the county, although the interior was over-restored by the Victorians. There is a brass to John Mordon (died 1410).

Fawley: St Mary. (Off A4155 north of Henley-on-Thames.)

The church was much restored for John Freeman of Fawley Court in 1748 and also in 1883. The most interesting features are the surviving fittings from the eighteenth-century restoration such as the font, panelling and pulpit, which were all brought from the Chandos mansion at Canons near Edgware. In the churchyard are two family mausolea: that of the Mackenzies, erected in 1862, and that of the Freemans, which dates from 1750.

Fenny Stratford: St Martin. (Off A5 just east of Bletchley.)

Originally built for Browne Willis between 1724 and 1731, the church was enlarged by William White in 1866 and was again expanded in 1908 and 1965. Browne Willis is buried in the church, his original floor slab now set in the east wall. The church is also the resting place of the 'Fenny Poppers' (see page 98).

Fingest: St Bartholomew. (Off B482 northwest of Marlow.)

This is one of the best-known of all Buckinghamshire churches because of its massive Norman tower, some 60 feet (18 metres) high and 27 feet (8 metres) square, with a later seventeenth- or eighteenth-century twin saddleback roof. It is of less interest internally through Victorian restoration but has a fourteenth-century font bowl and the royal arms of Queen Anne.

Gayhurst: St Peter. (Off B526 north-east of Newport Pagnell.)

An important example of the classical style, the church was rebuilt for George Wright, who also remodelled Gayhurst House, in 1728. A monument attributed to L. F. Roubiliac commemorates Wright's father, Sir Nathan Wright (died 1721), the Lord Keeper of the Great Seal, as well as Wright himself.

Great Hampden: St Mary Magdalene. (Between Princes Risborough and Great Missenden.)

The significance lies almost entirely in the connection with the Hampden family, who were associated with the parish from the eleventh century onwards. The earliest brass is to John Hampden (died 1496) and his wife while a later Sir John Hampden (died 1553) is depicted with two wives. John Hampden, the 'Patriot', had the south wall tablet erected to his wife, Elizabeth (died 1634), and is himself commemorated by a monument by Sir Henry Cheere. Hampden's actual burial place is unmarked and the monument by Cheere was erected in 1743 on the centenary of Hampden's death following the battle of Chalgrove Field.

Great Linford: St Andrew. (Between Wolverton and Newport Pagnell.)

The church is early fourteenth-century but with a chancel rebuilt in the early eighteenth century and Georgian internal fittings. There are brasses of the fifteenth and sixteenth centuries and a tablet to Sir William Pritchard (died 1704). Pritchard was responsible for erecting the nearby school and the almshouses, now renovated as small workshops for artists and craftsmen by the city of Milton Keynes (see page 48).

Hambleden: St Mary. (Off A4155 between Marlow and Henley-on-Thames.)

The church has been much rebuilt and restored at various periods, a new west tower being erected in 1721 to replace a Norman central tower which had collapsed eighteen years earlier. The monuments include one to Sir Cope D'Oyley (died 1633) but the main treasure is a large piece of early sixteenth-century carved oak panelling bearing the arms of Cardinal Wolsey and Richard Fox, Bishop of Winchester. Traditionally supposed to be part of Wolsey's bed, it may have come from The Vyne in Hampshire. The sea chest used by Lord Cardigan during the Crimean War is also in the church while W. H. Smith, first Lord Hambleden, is buried in the churchyard.

Hanslope: St James the Great. (North of Wolverton.)

The spire is regarded as the best of the few in the county. It was originally 200 feet (60 metres) high but was lowered when rebuilt after being struck by lightning in 1804. Inside, the chancel arch is Norman and the aisles thirteenth-century. There are fragments of wall paintings and a small brass to Mary Birchmore (died 1602). Later monuments include one to a bare-knuckle fighter, Alexander McKay (died 1830), and a man killed by his gamekeeper in 1912. The village has a Baptist chapel of 1809 and a Wesleyan chapel of 1826.

Hardwick: St Mary. (Off A413 north of Aylesbury.)

The north wall of the nave is almost certainly pre-Norman but the chancel was rebuilt

Left: *The church of St James the Great, Hanslope.*
Right: *St Peter's church, Gayhurst.*

by G. E. Street in 1873. An exterior monument was erected by Lord Nugent in 1818 at the reinterment of the remains of 247 bodies from Holman's Bridge, just outside Aylesbury. It was believed that these were victims of a 'Battle of Aylesbury' in November 1642 but the battle is a myth and the original burials were probably unconnected with the Civil War.

Hedgerley: St Mary. (Off A355 south-east of Beaconsfield.)

The church was entirely rebuilt by Benjamin Ferrey in 1852 and the interest lies in internal features brought from other churches. The seventeenth-century wooden pulpit comes from a church on Antigua destroyed by an earthquake in 1843, while a brass of 1540 is a fourteenth-century palimpsest previously used for an abbot of Bury St Edmunds in Suffolk. A framed fragment of red velvet is said to be from a cloak given as an altar cloth by King Charles II while a painting on the theme of the Ten Commandments dates from 1662.

High Wycombe: All Saints.

The south doorway and porch are the best examples of a number of Early English features of this, the second church built on the site. The upper part of an otherwise Perpendicular central tower was remodelled in Gothic style by Henry Keene in 1755 while both G. E. Street and J. O. Scott had a hand in Victorian restoration. The best monument is that to Henry Petty, Earl of Shelburne (died 1751), by Peter Scheemakers. The grave of the first Marquess of Lansdowne (see page 94) is unmarked. In the south transept is an eighteenth-century mayor's desk.

Churches and chapels

Hillesden: All Saints. (South of Buckingham.)

This was the church that inspired the young George Gilbert Scott, one of whose childhood architectural drawings is preserved in the vestry. Rebuilt in Perpendicular style by the monks of Notley Abbey in 1493, it was restored by Scott in 1875. The monuments are those of the Denton family, kinsmen of the Verneys. The former Denton mansion was next to the churchyard but was destroyed in the Civil War, rebuilt in 1648 and finally pulled down by the third Duke of Buckingham and Chandos in the late nineteenth century.

Ickford: St Nicholas. (Off A418 west of Thame.)

Mostly thirteenth-century, this church contains a tomb chest of Thomas Tipping (died 1595) with nine kneeling children and unusual Flemish 'Red Indian' style head-dresses above heads on the strapwork. In the easternmost side window of the north aisle is incised a nine men's morris board, now somewhat indistinct through a cement repair. A game played with coloured pegs, it was once immensely popular but relics of it are rare.

Iver: St Peter. (On B470 between Slough and Uxbridge.)

The north window is pre-Norman but the remainder of the church dates from the thirteenth and fourteenth centuries. A Norman font survives, and brasses of 1508, 1604 and 1610. A later monument is to Admiral Lord Gambier, while the churchyard has a memorial to a young naval midshipman, James Whitshed, killed while serving in the Mediterranean in 1813.

Jordans: Friends' Meeting House. (Off A40 east of Beaconsfield.)

See under Jordans (page 31).

Lathbury: All Saints. (Off B526 north of Newport Pagnell.)

Although originally ninth-century and with a Norman sculptured tympanum reset in the south aisle, the church is mostly fourteenth-century. One monument is to Margaret Andrews, who died in 1680 at the age of only fourteen before she could be married to the Duke of Somerset. An interesting brass to Richard Davies (died 1661) was erected by his son, who was Agent General for the English Nation on the west coast of Africa. The main feature, however, is the fifteenth-century wall paintings including a Doom, the Weighing of Souls and the Seven Sacraments.

Little Hampden: dedication unknown. (North-west of Great Missenden.)

This small church is important for its wall paintings. One of the two versions of St Christopher, that to the west of the doorway, is a particularly early example from the thir-

A Norman capital with dragons in All Saints' church, Lathbury.

The church of St John the Baptist, Little Missenden.

teenth century. Other saints also appear together with bishops and a lion and traces of a fifteenth-century Doom. Outside, the fifteenth-century timber-framed porch is noteworthy.

Little Horwood: St Nicholas. (North-east of Winslow.)

Although over-restored externally, with the exception of the Perpendicular west tower, the church is notable for its wall paintings. The image of St Nicholas is thirteenth-century and that of St Christopher is fifteenth-century, while the depiction of the Seven Deadly Sins as Pride and her daughters is early sixteenth-century.

Little Kimble: All Saints. (Off A4010 north of Princes Risborough.)

Like Little Horwood, this is a small church with notable wall paintings. An early fourteenth-century St Francis is shown preaching to the birds and there are also representations of St Bernard, St Clare, St George and St Catherine. In the chancel there is a series of thirteenth-century 'Chertsey' tiles with scenes from the romance of Sir Tristram.

Little Missenden: St John the Baptist. (Off

A413 west of Amersham.)

There are traces of pre-Norman work in the nave and chancel arch, a Norman 'Aylesbury' font and a range of wall paintings dating from the late twelfth to the fifteenth century. The largest shows St Christopher carrying the Christ Child but there are also scenes from the life of St Catherine and fragments of a Passion, Christ in Majesty, a Doom and the Seven Deadly Sins.

Maids Moreton: St Edmund. (On A413 north of Buckingham.)

Traditionally built for two maiden sisters of the Peover family, this is an important example of the Perpendicular style. There is a sixteenth-century wall painting of the Last Supper and a monument to Francis Atterbury, Bishop of Rochester (died 1685). One of the old church doors hung in the tower is pierced, so it is said, by Civil War bullet holes.

Marlow: All Saints.

The church was built by C. F. Inwood in 1832 but there are later additions by G. E. Street and a spire added by J. O. Scott in 1898. However, the internal monuments are from the older church that stood on the site. The most interesting is that to Sir Miles

Church of Christ the Cornerstone, Milton Keynes.

Hobart (died 1632), which illustrates the coaching accident in which he was killed on Holborn Hill. The showman John Richardson is buried in the churchyard and there is a memorial to his 'Spotted Boy' (died 1812), a white-spotted negro exhibited by Richardson.

Marlow: St Peter (Roman Catholic).
The church was built by Pugin between 1845 and 1848. It has a pleasant spire and displays what purports to be the embalmed hand of St James brought from Reading Abbey.

Milton Keynes (Central): Church of Christ the Cornerstone.
The first ecumenical city centre church in Britain, it is shared by the Anglican, Baptist, Methodist, Roman Catholic and United Reformed churches. Designed by Iain Smith, it was opened in 1992 and consists not only of the central worship area but also the Guild-

hall meeting place, a separate chapel, kitchen area and bookshop. A number of religious organisations are located in the surrounding offices of the complex, which is dominated by the dome and cross rising to 119 feet (36 metres) and representing the highest point in Milton Keynes. The cross itself is by Alan Evans and the stained glass under the dome by Alexander Beleshenko. For details of religious services and other facilities, contact Church of Christ the Cornerstone, 300 Saxon Gate West, Central Milton Keynes MK9 2ES. Telephone: 01908 237777.

Milton Keynes (village): All Saints. (Off A5130 south of Newport Pagnell.)
One of the best Decorated churches in the county, it is primarily of architectural interest, with delicate tracery and mouldings. There is a brass to Adam Babyngton (died 1427) and Victorian stained glass by Powell and Sons.

Moulsoe: Assumption. (South-east of Newport Pagnell.)
This mostly Decorated church has a brass of 1528 and monuments of the Carrington family. One commemorates the second Lord Carrington (died 1868), his grandson, Viscount Wendover, and thirty-six other members of the Royal Horse Guards killed at the second battle of Ypres in 1915. An Egyptian flag was taken during the 1882 Egyptian campaign by a Carrington. Their family graves lie behind a grilled enclosure in the churchyard.

Mursley: St Mary. (Off B4032 east of Winslow.)
Although much restored in 1867, the church retains the monuments of the Fortescue family of the long demolished Salden House. Sir John Fortescue (died 1607), who entertained Queen Elizabeth I at Salden and was the Queen's Chancellor of the Exchequer, has a monument, as do his wife Cecily (died 1570) and son Sir Francis Fortescue (died 1658).

North Crawley: St Firmin. (Off A422 between Newport Pagnell and Bedford.)
Only one other church in England is dedicated to St Firmin but the church is also interesting for its fifteenth-century rood

screen with sixteen panels depicting saints and prophets. The interior has Georgian fittings of pulpit and box pews.

Olney: St Peter and St Paul.

This largely fourteenth-century Decorated church has one of the few spires in Buckinghamshire. The roof of the nave was lowered in 1807. A window is dedicated to the memory of William Cowper and John Newton's grave is also here, having been brought from London in 1893.

Penn: Holy Trinity. (On B474 north-east of Beaconsfield.)

The church is mostly thirteenth-century but the interior has an eighteenth-century appearance with pews and pulpit brought from the Curzon family chapel in Mayfair. There are some post-Reformation brasses and Penn and Curzon monuments while windows commemorate two officers killed in the First World War. A Doom painted on oak boards in the fifteenth century is a rarity and the church also has a rare consecration cross. Four of the grandsons of William Penn are also buried here.

Pitstone: St Mary. Telephone enquiries: 01296 668806. (Off B488 north-east of Tring.)

Restored by the Redundant Churches Fund after it fell into disuse, the church has limited opening times. There are Norman features, an 'Aylesbury' font and mainly seventeenth-century internal fittings. A small fourteenth-century brass of a lady is possibly the earliest in the county.

Quainton: St Mary and Holy Cross. (Off A41 north-west of Aylesbury.)

The importance lies in its monuments. Brasses range from 1350 to 1510 while there are monuments to Richard Pigott (died 1635) by Giacomo Leoni, to Richard Winwood (died 1689) by Thomas Stayner, and to one of the translators of the Authorised Bible, Richard Brett (died 1637). A composite monument to three of the Dormer family and one to Mr Justice Dormer (died 1726), his wife and son are attributed to Roubiliac.

Ravenstone: All Saints. (Off B526 north-west of Newport Pagnell.)

A most notable monument commemorates Heneage Finch, first Earl of Nottingham (died 1682), Lord Chancellor to King Charles II. The south chapel was added especially for the monument. Finch also built the nearby almshouses.

Sherington: St Laud. (Off A509 north of Newport Pagnell.)

This is the only English church dedicated to St Laud. Primarily of architectural interest, it is a fine example of Decorated style with a central tower begun in the thirteenth century, but raised at a later date. The Congregational chapel in the village dates from 1822.

Soulbury: All Saints. (On B4032 west of Leighton Buzzard.)

The church is chiefly of interest for the Lovett monuments, of which the earliest is to Robert Lovett (died 1491). That to a later Robert Lovett (died 1699) is almost certainly

St Michael's church, Stewkley.

by Grinling Gibbons while that to Eleanor Lovett (died 1786) is in Coade stone by Coade and Seely.

Stewkley: St Michael. (On B4032 west of Leighton Buzzard.)

Regarded as one of the best examples of late Norman church architecture, this church escaped drastic restoration although G. E. Street did rebuild the south porch. Both externally and internally, a feature is the zigzag decoration.

Stoke Poges: St Giles. (Off B416 north of Slough.)

Best-known for its connections with Thomas Gray, who lies buried in the churchyard, the church is also notable for the sixteenth-century Hastings Chapel containing seventeenth-century stained heraldic glass. There is also a brass to Sir William Molyns (died 1425) and reminders of the Penn family.

West Wycombe: St Lawrence. (On A40 west of High Wycombe.)

The church was remodelled for Sir Francis Dashwood in the eighteenth century with an interior copied from the Sun Temple at Palmyra in Syria. It contains a version of 'The Last Supper' by Borgnis. On top of the tower is the golden ball in which Dashwood entertained John Wilkes and Charles Churchill.

Whaddon: St Mary. (Off A421 west of Bletchley.)

The arcades are earlier than the fourteenth-century chancel, chapel and tower. Inside there is the tomb of Sergeant Pigott (died 1519) with brass effigies and the plain tomb chest of Arthur, Lord Grey de Wilton (died 1593), who was the first Lord Lieutenant named solely for Buckinghamshire and also Lord Deputy in Ireland in the reign of Queen Elizabeth I. An interesting feature is an early weight-driven clock of 1673 by a local bellfounder, Anthony Chandler.

Whitchurch: St John Evangelist. (On A413 between Aylesbury and Winslow.)

Mostly late thirteenth- and early fourteenth-century, this is a large church with fragments of fourteenth-century heraldic glass and traces of fifteenth-century wall paintings. A poor-box of 1620 is an interesting feature while the monument to John Westcar (died

Willen church.

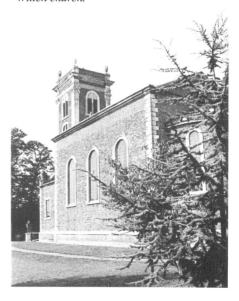

St Lawrence's church, West Wycombe.

Wing church.

1833) is striking with its representation of the prize bull he conveyed to market in London. The First World War memorial is also notable.

Willen: St Mary Magdalene. (North-east of Central Milton Keynes.)

Built for Dr Richard Busby, the headmaster of Westminster School, by Christopher Wren's assistant, Robert Hooke, between 1679 and 1680, this is the most complete and important classical-style church in the county.

Wing: All Saints. (On A418 between Aylesbury and Leighton Buzzard.)

One of the most important Anglo-Saxon churches in England, most of the apse, crypt, nave and aisles survive from the tenth century. The 'Aylesbury' font is twelfth-century. The monument to Sir Robert Dormer (died 1552) is one of the finest of its period. There are other Dormer monuments and brasses, one of which has an amusing rhyme for Thomas Cotes (died 1648), who was a porter in the Dormer household.

Winslow: Keach's Meeting House. Telephone: 01296 714181.

Off Market Walk is this Particular Baptist chapel of 1695 with complete original furnishings. Benjamin Keach (1640-1704) was a Baptist preacher at Winslow who was arrested in 1664 and placed in the pillory at both Winslow and Aylesbury. He left for London in 1668 long before the chapel was built. It is open to visitors by appointment.

Wotton Underwood: All Saints. (South of A41 between Aylesbury and Bicester.)

In this fourteenth-century church largely rebuilt by G. E. Street in 1867 a screen separates off the Grenville monuments. There is a brass of Edward Grenville (died 1585) and family tombs are arranged in tiers like drawers in a sideboard. In the aisle is a monument to the third (and last) Duke of Buckingham and Chandos (died 1889). Two members of the family do not lie here, prime ministers George Grenville (buried at Ludgershall) and Lord Grenville (buried at Burnham) (see page 94).

6
Historic buildings and gardens

The properties listed below (except for Chequers) are open to the public on a regular basis. Those opened only occasionally or those with gardens open on perhaps one or two days each year are not included. Chequers, which is not open to the public, is included because of its special interest. Opening times may vary and visitors are advised to contact the telephone numbers given for precise information.

Ascott House, Wing, Leighton Buzzard LU7 0PS. Telephone: 01296 688242. National Trust.
Open: house and gardens, April to May and September, Tuesday to Sunday; garden only, May to August, each Wednesday and last Sunday in month.

Incorporating an early seventeenth-century farmhouse, Ascott was enlarged by George Devey for Leopold de Rothschild, who acquired the property as a hunting box in 1874. It was again remodelled for Anthony de Rothschild in 1938. Its contents include Ming and K'ang Hsi porcelain, French furniture and fine paintings of the English, Italian, French and especially Dutch schools. The gardens by Veitch contain many specimen trees and shrubs chosen for their autumn foliage and a fountain group in bronze by the American sculptor Story, who also worked at Cliveden.

Boarstall Tower, Boarstall, Aylesbury HP18 9OX. National Trust.
Open by written appointment with tenant, May to September, Wednesdays.

The former three-storey gatehouse of a fourteenth-century fortified manor house, Boarstall Tower was much altered in the sixteenth and seventeenth centuries and survived the Civil War siege of Boarstall by Parliamentarian forces in June 1646, in which the original manor house and village were destroyed. The tower, which retains crossloops for archers, is surrounded by a moat and has a

3 acre (1.2 hectare) garden on the site of the manor house.

Buckingham Chantry Chapel, Market Hill, Buckingham. National Trust.
Open by written appointment with the Buckingham Heritage Trust Ltd, The Old Gaol, Market Hill, Buckingham MK18 1EW, from April to October.

One of the oldest buildings in the county, the Chantry Chapel of St John was originally built in the thirteenth century. Rebuilt in 1475, it was used as the Royal Latin School after the Reformation. It has a fine Norman doorway, fifteenth-century windows and seventeenth-century bench ends in the gallery but was otherwise restored by George Gilbert Scott in 1875.

Chenies Manor House, Chenies, Rickmansworth WD3 6ER. Telephone: 01494 762888.
Open April to September, Wednesdays, Thursdays and bank holiday Mondays.

Built between 1461 and 1523 to replace an older manor house, of which the thirteenth-century crypt remains, Chenies Manor House is Tudor in appearance. There are Tudor rooms, with contemporary tapestries and furniture, a reputed priest's hole, a doll collection and other special exhibitions including one on the history of kitchen gardens. The gardens surrounding the house include a physic garden, a penitential maze and a hedge maze.

The Great Fountain, Cliveden.

Chequers, Ellesborough, Aylesbury.

Although parts of the Chequers estate are crossed by public footpaths, the house itself and its immediate vicinity are closed to the public. A sixteenth-century house, it was presented to the nation by Lord Lee of Fareham in 1917 as a country residence for the Prime Minister in thanksgiving for Britain's deliverance during the First World War. Visible from the road from Great Missenden to Butlers Cross, and from the Ridgeway path, Chequers served as a prison for Lady Jane Grey's sister, Lady Mary, for two years. It also contains a unique collection of Cromwelliana acquired when it was in the possession of the Russell family, into which Oliver Cromwell's youngest daughter, Frances, married.

Chicheley Hall, Chicheley, Newport Pagnell MK16 9JJ. Telephone: 01234 391252.
Open Easter to May and August to September, Sundays and bank holiday Mondays.

Built between 1719 and 1723 by Francis Smith for Sir John Chester, Chicheley Hall is a fine example of Georgian architecture. It is noted for its fine panelling, its Palladian hall by Henry Flitcroft and a unique hidden library. Acquired by the Beatty family in 1952, the house now contains many memorabilia of Admiral of the Fleet Earl Beatty during his naval service and some of his collection of fine sea paintings. The gardens include a three-sided canal by George London.

Claydon House, Middle Claydon, Buckingham MK18 2EY. Telephone: 01296 730349 or 730693. National Trust.
Open April to October, Saturday to Wednesday and bank holiday Mondays.

Claydon is a mixture of the seventeenth-century house into which the Verney family moved in 1620, the eighteenth-century west front of a house begun by the second Earl Verney as a rival to Stowe, but unfinished when he went bankrupt in 1784, and the mid nineteenth-century remodelled south front. Much of the interior, however, is of the eighteenth century as executed for Earl Verney by Rose and Lightfoot, with extravagant decoration in the North Hall and Saloon, the upstairs Gothic Room and the extraordinary rococo fantasies of the Chinese Room. Many relics of the Verneys on display include Van Dyck portraits, a selection of the seventeenth-century muniments cataloguing the fortunes of a family divided by the Civil War, and items belonging to Florence Nightingale, the sister-in-law of Sir Harry Calvert, who inherited the property and assumed the name of Verney in the nineteenth century. Adjacent to the house is the church of All Saints, with sixteenth-century brasses of the Giffard family and seventeenth-century Verney monuments, including that to Sir Edmund Verney, the King's standard-bearer killed at the battle of Edgehill in 1642.

Cliveden, Taplow, Maidenhead SL6 0JA. Telephone: 01628 605069. National Trust.
Open: house (three rooms only), April to October, Thursday and Sunday; gardens, March to December, daily.

Occupying a magnificent position 200 feet (60 metres) above the Thames, the present house was built for the Duke of Sutherland by Sir Charles Barry after a fire in 1849. Further additions were made for the Duke of Westminster in 1870 and for the Astor family after 1893. The house will always be associated with the Astors and the 'Cliveden Set' but the first house was built on the site for the second Duke of Buckingham, whose duel with Lord Shrewsbury for the hand of Lady Shrewsbury in 1668 is commemorated in the garden terrace. Later the property was occupied by Frederick, Prince of Wales, in whose honour Thomas Arne's 'Rule Britannia' was first performed here in a masque in 1740 in a rustic amphitheatre. The house is now a luxury hotel, although some rooms are open to the public, but the glory of Cliveden lies in its 375 acres (151 hectares) of garden and woods hanging above the river and in the spectacular view of the Thames from Canning's Oak.

Dorney Court, Dorney, Windsor SL4 6QP. Telephone: 01628 604638.
Open June to September, Sundays, Mondays and Tuesdays, plus Easter weekend and Sundays and bank holiday Mondays in May.

Dating from about 1440, the house is a fine example of timber-framing with brick infilling although its exterior has been restored with the removal of later additions. Internally,

little has changed since the sixteenth century, with a magnificent great hall and gallery. The house has been in the possession of the Palmer family since the early seventeenth century. There are family portraits, needlework made for the marriage of Thomas Palmer in 1624 and a carved pineapple to commemorate the cultivation at Dorney of the first pineapple to be grown in England, which was presented to King Charles II by the gardener, John Rose, in 1661. The adjacent church of St James has wall paintings and an interesting monument to Sir William Garrard (died 1607) with his wife and fifteen children.

Apart from a pick your own fruit unit, the estate also now includes the Bressingham Plant Centre, which is open daily.

Dorneywood Garden, Dorneywood Road, Burnham, Slough SL1 8PY. National Trust.
Garden open by written appointment only with the Secretary, Dorneywood Trust, Dorneywood, Burnham SL1 8PY on two Wednesdays in July and two Saturdays in August.

Dorneywood has been an official residence for a Secretary of State since its gift to the nation by Lord Courtauld Thomson in 1942. The estate covers 215 acres (87 hectares) but only the gardens are open to the public.

Fawley Court, Henley-on-Thames RG9 3AE. Telephone: 01491 574917.
Open March to October, Wednesdays, Thursdays and Sundays.

On the site of the house of Bulstrode Whitelocke, damaged beyond repair during the Civil War, Fawley Court was rebuilt for William Freeman in 1684, possibly to a design by Wren. The exterior was later remodelled by James Wyatt and the gardens were redesigned by Lancelot 'Capability' Brown. It houses a museum devoted to Polish culture including armoury, manuscripts, paintings and militaria.

Hughenden Manor, High Wycombe HP14 4LA. Telephone: 01494 532580. National Trust.
Open: March, Saturdays and Sundays; April to October, Wednesdays to Sundays and bank

Hughenden Manor was Disraeli's home for over thirty years.

holiday Mondays.

The home of Benjamin Disraeli (see page 94) from 1847 until his death in 1881, the house was extensively altered during his occupation by the Gothic architect E. B. Lamb. The gardens were also transformed with a 'German forest' and a lake. Much of the interior is typically Victorian and remains largely as Disraeli knew it. Mementoes of the statesman are on display and there is an extensive collection of portraits of friends and contemporaries in the 'Gallery of Friendship'. Disraeli, his wife and Mrs Brydges Willyams are buried together in the churchyard of the church of St Michael, a fourteenth-century structure remodelled by Sir Arthur Blomfield between 1874 and 1890. It has a monument to Disraeli erected for Queen Victoria and a De Montfort Chapel faked by the Wellesbourne family in the sixteenth century as a means of claiming a pedigree.

Long Crendon Court House, Long Crendon, Aylesbury HP18 9AN. Telephone: 01844

Princes Risborough Manor House.

201096. National Trust.
Upper floor only open April to September, Wednesdays, Saturdays, Sundays and bank holiday Mondays.

One of the first buildings acquired by the National Trust, the Court House dates from the early fifteenth century and was originally a wool store or staple hall. The upper floor began to be used for the holding of manorial courts during the reign of Henry V. Its timber frame is infilled with brick, wattle and daub over a stone base.

Mentmore Towers, Mentmore, Leighton Buzzard LU7 0QH. Telephone: 01296 662183.
Open Sundays and bank holiday Mondays.

Another remarkable creation for the Rothschilds, the house was built between 1851 and 1854 for Baron Meyer de Rothschild by Sir Joseph Paxton and G. H. Stokes. The only surviving example of Paxton's domestic architecture, the house is modelled on the Elizabethan mansion of Wollaton in Nottinghamshire. It was noted for the early installation of hot-water heating and artificial ventilation. The contents were the subject of a controversial sale in 1977 and the house is now owned by the Transcendental Meditation Movement and is the central campus of Maharishi University of Natural Law.

Nether Winchendon House, Nether Winchendon, Aylesbury HP18 0DY. Telephone: 01844 290101.
Open daily from May Day bank holiday to late Spring bank holiday; also the Sunday and Monday of August bank holiday weekend.

Part of the endowment of Notley Abbey in the twelfth century, the house was acquired by Sir John Daunce, whose son married Elizabeth, daughter of Sir Thomas More. It was later acquired by the Tyringham family then in 1772 by the Bernards and has passed by family inheritance to the present owner. Papers on display relate to a previous owner, Sir Frances Bernard, Bt, last British governor of Massachusetts Bay. There are many medieval and Tudor features, including the drawing room. The house was extensively altered in the Strawberry Hill Gothick style at the end

The aviary at Waddesdon Manor.

of the eighteenth century. Fine furniture and family portraits as well as documents are on display.

Princes Risborough Manor House, Church Lane, Princes Risborough HP27 9AW. National Trust.
House and front garden open only by written appointment with the tenant, Wednesdays.

A limited number of rooms are open by written appointment. Features of the primarily seventeenth-century house are the Jacobean oak staircase and the drawing room with sixteenth-century fireplace. During the Second World War paintings from the National Gallery were stored in the house for safety.

Stowe Landscape Gardens, Stowe, Buckingham MK18 5EH. Telephone: 01280 813650 (house) or 822850 (gardens). National Trust.
House open during school spring and summer vacations, daily; gardens March to April, July to September, December to January, daily; April to July and September to October, Mondays, Wednesdays, Fridays and Sundays.

The original house on the site was built for Sir Richard Temple in the late seventeenth century but was then enlarged by Sir John Vanbrugh for Viscount Cobham in the early eighteenth century. Cobham's nephew, Earl Temple, altered the north front and in 1770 had the south front totally remodelled by his cousin, Thomas Pitt, to a design by Robert Adam. Within the house, the Marble Saloon, modelled on the Pantheon in Rome, dates from Temple's reconstruction, as does the Music Room in 'Pompeian' style by Valdre. However, the true glories of Stowe lie in the gardens, upon which three of the greatest English landscape gardeners worked in succession for Cobham and Temple – Charles Bridgeman, William Kent and 'Capability' Brown, who became head gardener at Stowe in 1741. Indeed, the gardens are a unique example of the successive stages in the eighteenth-century revolution in landscaping. They also contain a variety of garden temples and monuments including Kent's Temple of Ancient Virtue and Temple of British Worthies, James Gibbs's Gothic Temple and Temple of Friendship, and Thomas Pitt's Corinthian Arch dominating the skyline vista from the

Above: *The Gothic Temple is one of many splendid garden buildings at Stowe. The Temple is maintained by the Landmark Trust and can be hired for holidays.*

Opposite: *Stowe School is at the centre of one of the finest landscaped parks in Britain.*

south front. Opened as a school in 1923 after the final sale by the Grenvilles, Stowe also features modern additions by Clough Williams-Ellis and a 1927 school chapel by Sir Robert Lorimer.

Waddesdon Manor, Waddesdon, Aylesbury HP18 0JH. Telephone: 01296 651282 or 651211. National Trust.
House open April to October, Thursdays to Sundays and bank holiday Mondays. Gardens open March to December, Wednesdays to Sundays and bank holiday Mondays.
In the style of a French Renaissance château, Waddesdon Manor was built for Baron Ferdinand de Rothschild by the French architect Destailleur between 1874 and 1889. The bare Lodge Hill was planted with well-grown trees hauled up by teams of horses. The construction materials for the house were brought in on a specially built steam tramway which ran from Quainton Road station to Westcott. The extensive grounds include an aviary while the house displays rich collections of seventeenth- and eighteenth-century French decorative art: royal furniture, Savonnerie carpets, Sèvres and Meissen porcelain, tapestries, and silks woven specially for the house. The paintings are from the Dutch, Flemish, Italian and English schools, including portraits by Gainsborough. Reynolds and Romney. The Bachelors' Wing with European small arms, illuminated manuscripts and other works of art is open occasionally. Extensive restoration work completed in 1995 has included the opening for the first time of the wine cellars.

West Wycombe Park, West Wycombe, High Wycombe HP14 3AJ. Telephone: 01494 524411. National Trust.
House and gardens open June to August, Sundays to Thursdays; gardens only also in April and May, Sundays, Wednesdays and bank holiday Mondays.
A mid eighteenth-century Palladian mansion, West Wycombe was remodelled for Sir Francis Dashwood. A founder of the Society of Dilettanti in 1724, Dashwood was much influenced by Italian style and this is constantly echoed at West Wycombe with ceiling paintings after those by Carracci at the Palazzo Farnese and by Raphael at the Villa Farnesina. The park, with temples by Nicholas Revett, was partially redesigned by Humphry Repton, the one great landscape gardener not represented at Stowe. The village of West Wycombe is also owned by the National Trust, as is Church Hill and its iron age camp that surrounds the church and Dashwood mausoleum (see page 93).

Winslow Hall, Winslow, Buckingham MK18 3HL. Telephone: 01296 712323.
Open bank holiday weekends; July to August, Wednesdays and Thursdays; and by written appointment on other occasions.
Almost certainly designed by Sir Christopher Wren, the house was built for Sir William Lowndes, then Secretary of the Treasury, in 1700. Woodwork was executed by the king's joiner and carpenter, Hopson and Bankes, and the gardens were laid out by the king's gardeners, Wise and London. The house contains early eighteenth-century furniture, *objets d'art*, bibelots, jade and Chinese art of the Tang period.

Wotton House, Wotton Underwood, Aylesbury HP18 0SB. Telephone: 01844 238363.
Open August and September, Wednesdays.
Similar to the original design for Buckingham House (now Buckingham Palace), Wotton was built for Richard Grenville in 1704 but internally remodelled by Sir John Soane after being gutted by a disastrous fire in 1820. After the house was saved from demolition in 1957, Soane's work, including delicate cornices, was found to be intact beneath 1929 alterations and has been restored. The house retains its original eighteenth-century wrought iron balustrade by Tijou and stonework by Gibbons, including the probably unique portico to the west door. The park was originally laid out by George London in 1704 but redesigned by 'Capability' Brown in 1757-60.

7
Museums

The number of museums in the county has grown in recent years and they range from the more traditional and the literary to new specialised collections. A further museum is planned at Bletchley Park (see page 15).

Amersham

Amersham Museum, 49 High Street, Amersham HP7 0DP. Telephone: 01494 725754 or 724299.

Opened in its present location, a building dating back to the fifteenth century, in 1991, the museum has an expanding collection of local interest ranging from the prehistoric to the present. The museum won the National Heritage Museum of the Year Award in 1993.

Aylesbury

Buckinghamshire County Museum, Church Street, Aylesbury HP20 2QP. Telephone: 01296 696012 or 88849.
Open Mondays to Saturdays (except bank holiday Mondays).

In the oldest part of Aylesbury, the museum occupies a handsome group of mainly Georgian buildings, one of which is the old Grammar School of 1720. A mid eighteenth-century plaster ceiling in Ceeley House is of interest as well as the medieval roof timbers exposed in another part of the house. The museum is undergoing major renovation and only two galleries are open to the public. However, the Aylesbury Gallery is an imaginative display of the development of the town. The Special Exhibitions Gallery has a changing programme of displays. The museum is due to reopen fully in October 1995, adopting 'a totally new and innovative approach to local history'. It will contain the Roald Dahl Gallery, featuring many of the author's characters and a Regional Art Gallery with space to display major temporary exhibitions as well as the museum's important art and craft collections.

Beaconsfield

Royal Army Educational Corps Museum, Wilton Park, Beaconsfield HP9 2RP. Telephone: 01494 683271.
Open by appointment only.

Access is restricted as the museum is inside a military establishment and it is necessary to telephone for an appointment. The museum illustrates the development of army education since 1800 and contains material relating to the Corps of Army Schoolmasters, founded in 1846, as well as to the Royal Army Educational Corps. The work of the corps overseas is especially featured.

Buckingham

The Old Gaol Museum, Market Hill, Buckingham MK18 1EW.
Open April to September and November to December, Monday to Wednesday, Friday to Saturday, and Sunday afternoons.

Built in 1748 in Gothic style, the Old Gaol was constructed as part of the attempt to bring the assizes back to the town from Aylesbury. It ceased to be a lock-up at the end of the nineteenth century and was opened as a museum by the Buckingham Heritage Trust in 1993. The first phase of development includes an audio-visual presentation on the Old Gaol itself, collections of local interest from prehistoric to Edwardian times and the collection of the Buckinghamshire Military Museum Trust, devoted to the auxiliary military units raised in the county such as militia, yeomanry and volunteers. There are also temporary exhibitions. Subsequent development will concentrate on portraying the history of the town.

Chalfont St Giles

Chiltern Open Air Museum, Newland Park, Gorelands Lane, Chalfont St Giles HP8 4AD. Telephone: 01494 871117 or 872163.

Winslow Hall is built around its four magnificent chimneys.

Chicheley Hall contains mementoes of Admiral of the Fleet Earl Beatty.

Milton's Cottage at Chalfont St Giles was the poet's refuge from the Great Plague 1665.

Open April to October, Wednesdays to Sundays and bank holiday Mondays.

Historic buildings from the Chilterns area, some as much as five hundred years old, have been saved from demolition and re-erected here. The collection includes a baker's flour granary from Wing, the old toll house from High Wycombe, barns and cart sheds on a 44 acre (18 hectare) site. There are occasional special events.

Milton's Cottage and Museum, Deanway, Chalfont St Giles HP8 4JH. Telephone: 01494 872313.
Open March to October, Wednesdays to Sundays, and bank holiday Mondays.

John Milton came to Chalfont St Giles in June 1665 to escape the Plague in London and lived in this cottage until returning to the capital in the following spring. *Paradise Lost* was completed here and *Paradise Regained* was begun. Contemporary relics of Milton are displayed as well as rare books and exhibits of local interest. There is a charming and well-stocked cottage garden.

High Wycombe

Booker Aircraft Museum, Wycombe Air Park, Booker, High Wycombe. Telephone: 01494 452320.
Open weekends throughout the year.

One of fifteen wartime airfields in Buckinghamshire, Booker now displays aircraft under restoration and artefacts from excavations of aircraft that crashed in the Chiltern area during the Second World War. Static exhibits include a Vampire T11, a Provost T1, a Whirlwind Fairy, a Nord (Me 108) and a Hunter T53.

Wycombe Local History and Chair Museum, Castle Hill House, Priory Avenue, High Wycombe HP13 6PX. Telephone: 01494 421895.
Open Mondays to Saturdays (except bank holidays).

The museum is situated in an eighteenth-century house set in attractive and historic grounds. Displays explore the history of the Wycombe area, focusing on a unique collection of country chairs, linked trades such as

The wireless display at the Milton Keynes Museum of Industry and Rural Life.

caning and rushing and other objects of local interest. There are temporary exhibitions on a variety of subjects which change every month, activities for children and some special events at weekends.

Milton Keynes

City Discovery Centre at Bradwell Abbey, Alston Drive, Bradwell Abbey, Milton Keynes MK13 9AP. Telephone: 01908 227229.

On the site of a twelfth-century Benedictine priory, the City Discovery Centre provides information and education services on the development of the new city and its historical and natural environments. The centre itself is in a sixteenth-century farmhouse while the 22 acre (9 hectare) site also includes the fourteenth-century shrine to Our Lady of Bradwell, a fourteenth-century cruck barn, medieval fishponds and a reconstructed and fully organic herb garden. The centre runs a lively public events programme and details about this, school and study programmes and the resource collection can be obtained from the centre. The abbey is located off the Stacey Bushes/H3 Monks Way roundabout (A422).

Milton Keynes Exhibition Gallery, Milton Keynes Central Library, 555 Silbury Boulevard, Central Milton Keynes MK9 3HL. Telephone: 01908 835025.
Open Mondays to Saturdays (except bank holidays).

The gallery has some ten exhibitions each year, often relating to arts and crafts, but ranging from the historical to the contemporary.

Milton Keynes Museum of Industry and Rural Life, Stacey Hill Farm, Southern Way, Wolverton, Milton Keynes MK12 5EJ. Telephone: 01908 316222.
Open Easter to October, Wednesdays to Sundays and bank holiday Mondays.

Aiming to preserve aspects of the past that have disappeared with the coming of the new city, the collection contains domestic, agricultural and industrial material from the north of the county with an emphasis on working exhibits. There are workshops of many trades, including those of the wheelwright, printer and cobbler and a blacksmith's forge. A farmhouse kitchen and Victorian parlour portray domestic life whilst an extensive range of agricultural equipment shows the work of the farmer. Other displays cover industrial engines, photography, electrical equipment and wirelesses, lawnmowers, the dairy, bakery, laundry and a working waterwheel. There are also relics of the Wolverton and Stony Stratford Tramway.

Olney

Cowper and Newton Museum, Orchard Side, Market Place, Olney MK46 4AJ. Telephone: 01234 711516.
Open February to mid December, Tuesdays to Saturdays and bank holiday Mondays.

The museum is dedicated to the memory of the poet and hymnwriter William Cowper, who lived in the house from 1768 to 1786. Here many of his best-known poems and hymns were written, including 'John Gilpin' and 'God Moves in a Mysterious Way'. Many of Cowper's personal possessions and furniture are displayed in the house along with those of his evangelical friend John Newton, who was curate of Olney from 1764 to 1780 and wrote 'Amazing Grace' and many other much loved hymns. Cowper's works contain many references to the house and to his summerhouse, which is to be found in one of the two delightful gardens. Lacemaking was once the economic mainstay of many Olney families, and a fine collection of lace is displayed in the house where Cowper's servant used to live. There are also local history and bygone collections on show.

Pitstone

Pitstone Green Farm Museum, Vicarage Road, Pitstone, Leighton Buzzard LU7 9EY. Telephone: 01296 661997 (general) or 668083 (parties). Off the B489, 3 miles (5 km) north-east of Tring.
Open May to September, last Sunday in the month and bank holiday afternoons; also special craft open days, second Sundays in June, July and September.

Opening times are limited here but a visit is well worthwhile since several thousand rural and domestic bygones of local interest are attractively displayed by the Pitstone Local History Society against the background of a workshop and domestic settings. The Pitstone Local History Society also leases Ford End Watermill at Ivinghoe nearby (see page 89).

Pitstone Windmill, standing in a field near Ivinghoe, is possibly the oldest surviving in Britain.

Opposite: *The herb garden at Bradwell Abbey in Milton Keynes.*

8
Industrial archaeology

The county is not traditionally associated with heavy industry and its industrial past reflects rurally based industries such as chairmaking and lacemaking. However, the communications of the nineteenth century have left their mark, with canal and railway relics being the most obvious features of the industrial age to survive in the landscape.

Canals first appeared in Buckinghamshire in the late eighteenth century, the Grand Junction Canal (now the Grand Union) being begun in 1793 to provide a more direct route between the Thames and Birmingham. It was not completed until 1805 and even then the difficulty of crossing the Ouse was not fully overcome until the construction of the 'Iron Trunk' at Wolverton in 1811. Branches were eventually opened to Aylesbury, Buckingham, Newport Pagnell, Slough and Wendover, the Slough branch as late as 1882. Many of the locks were subsequently duplicated in order to speed the traffic to compete with the railways. Many parts of the canal system are now overgrown but there are particularly fine locks at Marsworth and Soulbury.

The first railway route driven through the county was the London & Birmingham Railway, passing through Cheddington, Bletchley and Wolverton, and built between 1835 and 1838. The cutting at Ivinghoe reaches a depth of 57 feet (17 metres) for over a quarter of a mile (400 metres) while the major embankments at Cheddington and Wolverton are notable for their length and height respectively. Later part of the London & North Western Railway Company, the company purchased land at Wolverton in 1837 and created a new town around its locomotive and carriage works. Wolverton remains dominated by railway architecture. The second route brought through Buckinghamshire was the Great Western Railway Company line from London to Bristol in 1838, built despite opposition from Eton College.

Other parts of the railway network constructed in the county were essentially link lines. One of the most interesting was the Brill Tramway, recalled by the name Tramway Hill in Brill. It was originally built to convey workers and livestock from Quainton Road station to the estate of the third Duke of Buckingham and Chandos at Wotton Underwood in 1870 and extended to Brill in 1872. It closed in 1935 and the route can be followed along a new 6 mile (10 km) long Tramway Trail. At the very end of the nineteenth century the Metropolitan and Great Central line linked London to Sheffield through Aylesbury and, in the early years of the twentieth century a new line from Paddington to Birmingham was routed through High Wycombe. The later routes were probably most significant for their stimulation of the growth of 'Metroland'.

Mills were once one of the most common features in the landscape. In 1086, for example, Domesday Book listed seventy-eight mills in the county while the Posse Comitatus of 1798 recorded no less than 122. At first most were water-driven and a windmill located at Worminghall in the mid twelfth century is one of the earliest recorded in the whole of western Europe. Most kinds of windmill are still represented and, besides the watermill at Ford End (details below), there is also that at Hambleden, although this is a private residence not open to the public.

Brill Windmill.

Bradwell Tower Mill, New Bradwell, Milton Keynes (OS 152: SP 831412).

Built about 1816 of local limestone, the windmill continued in use until 1871. It has a cap of the traditional 'upturned boat' shape and an elevated walkway for tending the sails. The mill is operated through a universally joined rod system of turning gear. The mill is still undergoing restoration.

Brill Windmill, Brill Common, Brill, Aylesbury (OS 165: SP 652142). Telephone enquiries: 01844 237724.
Open Sunday afternoons and by arrangement.

There has been a windmill at Brill since the thirteenth century and there were still two in existence until 1906. The surviving mill, a weatherboarded post mill with brick-protected base, dates from 1668 and was in use until 1916.

Buckinghamshire Railway Centre, Quainton Road Station, Quainton, Aylesbury HP22 4BY. Telephone: 01296 655450.
Steaming days: April to October, Sundays and bank holidays, plus Wednesdays from June to August. Non-steaming days (open for static viewing only): April to October, Saturdays; November and January to March, Sundays.

Quainton Road Station was opened by the Aylesbury and Buckingham Railway Company in 1868, later becoming a station on the Metropolitan and Great Central line. There are still freight trains on the line, enabling the Quainton Railway Preservation Society collection to be reached by train from Aylesbury on special occasions. At Quainton the centre houses one of the largest private collections of railway engines and rolling stock. Over thirty engines include the Great Western's *King Edward I* and there is the opportunity to see restoration work taking place as well as to ride on steam-hauled trains. The museum features local railways, while a special exhibition concentrates on industrial railways.

Denbigh Hall Bridge, Fenny Stratford (OS 152: SP 864353).

This is where the former London & Birmingham Railway main line crosses over Watling Street (A5). Until the line was completed in September 1838 passengers for Birmingham alighted at the bridge and travelled

Visitors watch a demonstration of iron age domestic life at the Chiltern Open Air Museum.

At Bletchley, the Fenny Poppers are fired each year on St Martin's Day, 11th November.

by horse-drawn coach to rejoin the railway at Rugby. A plaque erected on the south side of the bridge in 1920 commemorates this arrangement.

Ford End Watermill, Station Road, Ivinghoe, Leighton Buzzard LU7 9EA. Telephone enquiries: 01582 600391 (general) or 01296 668083 (parties).
Open May to September, Sundays and bank holiday afternoons, with milling on certain days.

Recorded as working in 1798 but probably much older, this small mill was in use until 1963. Now restored to working order, it retains the atmosphere of a typical country mill in the late nineteenth century. It incorporates an unusual sheep wash.

Great Linford Brick Kilns, Great Linford Park, Milton Keynes (OS 152: SP 859415).

Within Great Linford Manor House Park, these two restored brick kilns date from the end of the nineteenth century and were built by George Osborn Price of Newport Pagnell. An information panel explains their use.

Ickford Bridge, Ickford (OS 165: SP 649065).

Spanning the river Thame and the border with Oxfordshire on the road to Tiddington, this bridge dates from 1685.

The Iron Trunk aqueduct, Wolverton (OS 152: SP 800418).

Initially a series of locks was envisaged as a means of carrying the Grand Junction Canal across the Ouse valley between Cosgrove and Wolverton but in 1799 the engineer, James Barnes, suggested that an aqueduct would prevent the locks being flooded. A masonry aqueduct by William Jessop was opened in August 1805 but collapsed in February 1808. A temporary wooden structure was then replaced by the present cast-iron trunk, opened on 21st January 1811.

Lacey Green Windmill, Windmill Farm, Lacey Green (OS 165: SP 819009). Telephone enquiries: 01844 343560.
Open May to September, Sundays and bank holiday Mondays.

The mill at Lacey Green, near Princes Risborough, is thought to be the oldest surviving smock mill in England. Originally erected at Chesham in 1650, it was moved to its present site in 1821. It has been under restoration by the Chiltern Society for some years.

Maidenhead Railway Bridge, Taplow (OS 175: SU 902811).

Built by Isambard Kingdom Brunel in 1838 to carry the Great Western Railway over the river Thames between Taplow in Buckinghamshire and Maidenhead in Berkshire, this bridge has one of the largest brickwork spans ever built and was painted by Turner in the foreground of his 'Rain, Steam and Speed'.

Marlow Bridge, Marlow (OS 175: SU 852861).

The suspension bridge over the Thames at Marlow dates from 1832 and is the work of W. T. Clarke, who later designed bridges at Budapest in Hungary and Hammersmith in London.

Olney Bridge, Olney (OS 152: SP 888508).
This important bridge over the Great Ouse

Lacey Green windmill.

dates from the eighteenth century.

Pitstone Windmill, Ivinghoe, Leighton Buzzard (OS 165: SP 946158). Telephone enquiries: 01296 668227. National Trust.
Open May to September, Sundays and bank holidays.

This post mill is reputed to be Britain's oldest surviving windmill, one timber being dated 1627, although the mill has been restored and rebuilt extensively since. It remained in use until 1902, when it was damaged in a storm, but is now fully restored.

Quainton Windmill, 16 The Green, Quainton, Aylesbury (OS 165: SP 747204). Telephone: 01296 655348.
Open Sunday mornings and by request.

Built about 1830 with bricks made on the site, it was constructed for James Anstiss. A

tower mill, it is 65 feet (20 metres) high ar has six floors. It is under restoration.

Thornborough Bridge, Thornborough (C 165: SP 730332).

Off the A421 between Buckingham ar Bletchley, this is the oldest surviving brid; in the county. Some 12 feet (3.7 metres) wid it may well date from the fourteenth centur There is a car park with interpretative ar picnic facilities and the bridge is the startir point of a 4 mile (6 km) circular walk.

Tickford Bridge, Newport Pagnell (OS 15 SP 878438).

The oldest iron bridge still in daily u spans the river Lovat and was opened in 181 Cast by Walkers of Rotherham, it is one only two open-frame voussoir types in exi ence, the other being in Jamaica.

Marlow suspension bridge.

9
Other places to visit

Bekonscot Model Village, Warwick Road, Beaconsfield HP9 2PL. Telephone: 01494 672919.
Open mid February to end of October, daily.
The famous model village of Bekonscot was started by Roland Callingham in 1929 in what was then merely a muddy field. There are now over 160 buildings and 2500 figures in the attractively landscaped site of over 40,000 square feet (3716 square metres), which includes castles, churches, a race-course, a zoo and villages. The name derives from Beaconsfield and from Ascot, which was the home of the designer of the miniature railway. The railway has 7000 feet (2100 metres) of track with twelve engines and thirty coaches and wagons. Often visited by royalty, the village has raised enormous sums for charity and is particularly linked with the Church Army.

Boarstall Duck Decoy, Boarstall, Aylesbury. Telephone: 01844 237488. National Trust.
Open April to August, Wednesdays, Saturdays, Sundays and bank holiday Mondays.
Managed for the National Trust by BBONT, this is one of only three remaining examples in Britain of an eighteenth-century working duck decoy. Designed to lure birds into 'pipes', a decoy provided a source of winter meat, in this instance for the Aubrey family of Boarstall Tower (see page 70), for whom it was built between 1700 and 1750. There are interpretative displays and working demonstrations while the 13 acre (5.3 hectare) woodland site also has a lake and a nature trail. Today the pipe is used by the ornithologists for catching migrating duck so that they can be ringed and scientifically recorded. They are then immediately released.

Bucks Goat Centre, Layby Farm, Stoke Mandeville, Aylesbury HP22 5XJ. Telephone: 01296 612983. Off the A4010 between Stoke Mandeville and Princes Risborough.
Open Tuesdays to Sundays and bank holidays.
This is the most comprehensive collection of goats in Britain and also has other livestock and a pets' corner. The Information Centre has facilities for talks and seminars and there are a farm shop and a plant nursery specialising in shrubs.

Chalfont Shire Horse Centre, Model Farm, Gorelands Lane, Chalfont St Giles HP8 4AB. Telephone: 01494 872304.
Open daily, March to September.
Almost fifty Shire horses can be seen together with a fine collection of heavy horse harnesses and a carriage museum which includes London horse buses, show drays and farm wagons. There are also a blacksmith's shop, children's play area and pets' corner.

The Chiltern Brewery, Nash Lee Road, Terrick, Aylesbury HP17 0TQ. Telephone: 01296 613647. Off the B4009.
Open Mondays to Saturdays.
This traditional brewery opened in 1980. There is a small brewery museum and visitors may view the brewing rooms.

Fenny Lodge Gallery, 72 Simpson Road, Bletchley, Milton Keynes MK1 1BD. Telephone: 01908 642207.
Open Mondays to Saturdays.
Attractively set in an eighteenth-century house at Fenny Lock on the Grand Union Canal, the Gallery displays paintings, ceramics, sculpture, jewellery and free-blown glass.

West Wycombe mausoleum.

Glass Craft, Broad Lane, Wooburn Green, High Wycombe HP10 0LL. Telephone: 01494 671033.
Open Tuesdays to Sundays and bank holiday Mondays.

This is a glass craft centre, established in a converted barn, which demonstrates glassblowing, stained glassmaking and other techniques. Short courses, including one for beginners, are offered in glass crafts.

Grebe Canal Cruises, Pitstone Wharf, Pitstone, Leighton Buzzard LU7 9AD. Telephone: 01296 661920 (day) or 01628 472500 (evening).
Cruises operate April to early October at weekends; also on weekdays during Easter week, Spring bank holiday week, and late July to August bank holiday.

Regular scheduled 1½ hour cruises in all-weather boats with bars run along a beautiful stretch of the Grand Union Canal from Pitstone Wharf to Marsworth and back. Longer, 5½ hour cruises run on certain days.

Home of Rest for Horses, Westcroft Stables, Speen Farm, Slad Lane, Lacey Green, Princes Risborough. Telephone: 01494 488464.
Open daily.

A registered charity, the home cares for horses, ponies and donkeys and provides visitors with the opportunity to see equine welfare work in progress. Cavalry and police horses are among the residents, which formerly included Sefton, the Household Cavalry horse injured in the Hyde Park bomb attack.

Oak Farm Rare Breeds Park, Broughton, Aylesbury HP22 5AW. Telephone: 01296 415709.
Open Easter to August, Sunday, Wednesday, Thursday, Friday and bank holidays; September and October, Sunday only.

This is a traditional livestock farm with sheep, goats, cattle, pigs and poultry and includes many rare breeds. Most of the animals can be approached and petted or fed by visitors.

Odds Farm Park Rare Breeds Centre, Wooburn Common, High Wycombe HP10 0LG. Telephone: 01628 520188.
Open April to October, daily. Telephone for daily events.

This is a friendly family-run farm with rare and interesting breeds of livestock. Most animals can be hand-fed and there are plenty of other hands-on experiences for children to enjoy, including bottle-feeding and milking the goats. The animals include cattle, pigs, ponies, ducks, poultry, guinea-pigs and rabbits. There are picnic and play areas, pets' corner, craft shop and tea rooms.

Weston Underwood Flamingo Gardens and Zoological Park, Manor House, Weston Underwood, Olney. Telephone: 01234 711451.
Open April to June, Sundays and Wednesdays; July to September, weekends, Wednesdays, Thursdays and bank holidays.

Located in what was once the estate of the Throckmortons, the family which befriended William Cowper when he moved to Weston from Olney in 1786, the gardens were originally the home of Christopher Marler's specialised collection of wildfowl. They now have over a hundred species of birds and mammals, including swans, ducks, geese, storks, flamingoes, bison, alpacas, white wallabies and seven species of pelican.

West Wycombe Caves and Mausoleum, West Wycombe Hill Road, West Wycombe, High Wycombe HP14 3AJ. Telephone: 01494 524411 or 533739.
Open March to May, weekdays, Sundays and bank holidays; May to October, daily; November, Sundays.

Although not owned by the National Trust, the Mausoleum and Caves are nonetheless closely linked to West Wycombe Park and the grand design of Sir Francis Dashwood. Erected in 1765 with a bequest of £500, the Mausoleum echoes Constantine's Arch in Rome and principally commemorates Dashwood's wife, although the heart of the poet Paul Whitehead was also buried there. Down the hill is the entrance to the Caves, excavated between 1748 and 1752 to provide chalk foundations for the road laid out between West Wycombe and High Wycombe. The caves now contain tableaux depicting Dashwood and his friends, who were members of the Hell Fire Club, and others associated with West Wycombe, including Benjamin Franklin, who visited here. The church of St Lawrence stands at the top of Church Hill (see page 68).

Wickenden Vineyards, Wickenden, Cliveden Road, Taplow, Maidenhead. Telephone: 01628 29455.
Open by appointment: groups of eighteen or more welcome.

Established since 1976, this 4 acre (1.6 hectare) site has over five thousand vines and produces English table wine. Visitors can see grape crushing and filtering in the winery.

10
A Buckinghamshire biography

Six British prime ministers have connections with Buckinghamshire, five of them being buried in the county. The Earl of Shelburne, later first **Marquess of Lansdowne** (1737-1805), prime minister in 1782-3, was responsible for a number of buildings in High Wycombe and resided at Wycombe Abbey. He is buried without monument in the family vault at High Wycombe's church of All Saints. His successor as prime minister, William Bentinck, third **Duke of Portland** (1738-1809), held the office in both 1783 and from 1807 to 1809, residing at Bulstrode Park, Gerrards Cross, where he died. Portland's immediate predecessor when he took office for the second time was William Wyndham Grenville, **Lord Grenville** (1759-1834). Grenville was prime minister from 1806 to 1807 and was the son of another prime minis-

ter, **George Grenville** (1712-70), who held the office from 1763 to 1765. George Grenville, who is best-known as the man who imposed Stamp Duty on the American colonies, was of the Grenville family of Wotton House and Stowe and is buried at St Mary's church, Ludgershall. It was his eldest brother, Richard, Earl Temple, who inherited the Stowe estate through marriage with the Temple heiress in 1749. Thus both Stowe and Wotton passed into the possession of the Grenvilles while Lord Grenville purchased the Dropmore estate in 1792 and is buried in the church of St Peter at Burnham. One of the Grenville descendants, the third (and last) Duke of Buckingham and Chandos (1823-89), was a patron of the best-known of all Buckinghamshire prime ministers, **Benjamin Disraeli** (1804-81). Disraeli, later Earl of

Hughenden church, the burial place of Benjamin Disraeli.

Beaconsfield, lived as a child at Bradenham and purchased Hughenden Manor in 1848. Member of Parliament for the county from 1847 until his elevation to the peerage in 1875, Disraeli was prime minister from 1874 to 1880 and is buried at Hughenden. He is also associated with the Red Lion in the High Street at High Wycombe, from the original portico of which he made an election address in 1832, and he is commemorated by a statue in Aylesbury Market Square. The sixth prime minister is **Lord John Russell** (1792-1878), who held the office from 1846 to 1852 and was buried in the family chapel at Chenies.

To some extent, Disraeli's friendship arrested the decline of the Grenvilles, whose fortunes were squandered on Stowe. Although the final sale of Stowe did not take place until 1921, there had been an earlier bankruptcy in 1848. One of the chief beneficiaries of the sale of Grenville lands was the Rothschild family, who began large-scale purchases in the 1840s. Nathan Meyer, first Lord Rothschild, established his estate at Tring in Hertfordshire but within Buckinghamshire the mansions remain of **Baron Meyer de Rothschild** (1818-74) at Mentmore, **Leopold de Rothschild** (1845-1917) at Ascott, **Baron Ferdinand de Rothschild** (1839-98) at Waddesdon Manor and **Baron Alfred de Rothschild** (1842-1918) at Halton. Halton is occupied by the Royal Air Force and neither this house nor a pavilion built for Alice de Rothschild at Eythrope in 1883 are open to the public. A fifth Rothschild mansion, that of Sir Anthony de Rothschild (1810-76) at Aston Clinton, has been demolished.

If prime ministers could be said to represent the political establishment, the Rothschilds, in breaching political and religious discrimination, fell within a Buckinghamshire tradition of fostering political and religious dissent. The founder of the Lollards, **John Wycliffe** (1320-84), held the living of Ludgershall from 1368 to 1372 although he was never resident there. Amersham is especially associated with Lollard and later Protestant martyrdom. Bury Farm and Woodside Farm at Amersham were Quaker centres, the former being connected with the Penningtons and the latter with **Gulielma Springett**, who

became the first wife of **William Penn**. Penn (1641-1718), the founder of Pennsylvania, is recalled at Penn but may have few connections with the original family of that name in the parish. However, he and his wife and other leading Quakers are best-known for their association with Jordans. The Quaker families of Pennington and Ellwood are also linked to **John Milton** (1608-74). Milton resided briefly at Chalfont St Giles and earlier he had lived at Horton between 1632 and 1640, the parish being one of those transferred to Berkshire in 1974.

Milton's cottage was one of the few properties to remain in the hands of the Fleetwood family after the restoration of King Charles II. The Fleetwoods, like many other Buckinghamshire families, had fought for Parliament and Milton himself escaped punishment for his association with Cromwell only through the intercession of powerful friends. Another affected by the Civil War was the poet

Middle Claydon church: Sir Edmund Verney's tomb.

Great Hampden church.

John Hampden's statue in Market Square, Aylesbury.

Edmund Waller (1606-87). Born at Coleshill, now in Buckinghamshire but then a detached parish of Hertfordshire, Waller is buried in the churchyard of St Mary and All Saints, Beaconsfield, close to his estate of Hall Barn. Implicated in a Royalist conspiracy, Waller fled the country and did not return from exile to Hall Barn until 1651. The divisions of the war are also powerfully recalled by the experience of the Verney family of Claydon House. **Sir Edmund Verney** (1590-1642) died defending the King's Standard at Edgehill but his eldest son, Ralph, supported Parliament. The Verneys were linked by kinship to the Denton family of Hillesden, the church at which still has reminders of the war, as has nearby Steeple Claydon. It was the Civil War, too, that resulted in the death of one of the county's best-known historical figures, **John Hampden**.

Hampden (1595-1643) will always be remembered for his stand against the imposition of Ship Money in 1635. The family home was Hampden House at Great Hampden, where the church of St Mary Magdalene has a monument to the 'Patriot'. The land on which Hampden refused to pay twenty shillings Ship

Money was then in the parish of Stoke Mandeville but now lies in Prestwood, where a monument commemorates the deed. A facsimile of the Ship Money document hangs in the church of St Nicholas at Great Kimble, where Hampden made his refusal public. He is also recalled both by a window of 1902 in the church of St John the Baptist at The Lee and by a statue in Aylesbury.

Hampden's name conjures up the notion of liberty rather more readily than that of **John Wilkes** (1727-97), who was also associated with the ideal. Member of Parliament for Aylesbury from 1757 to 1764, Wilkes lived at Prebendal House, Aylesbury, adjacent to St Mary's church. A plaque in the churchyard was erected by Wilkes to the memory of his gardener and there are relics of Wilkes in the Buckinghamshire County Museum nearby. His notorious lifestyle is recalled at West Wycombe Caves, where he was a member of the Hell Fire Club formerly associated with Medmenham Abbey. A contemporary of Wilkes was a man of equal independence of thought and one of the greatest of political philosophers, **Edmund Burke** (1730-97). Member of Parliament for Wendover from 1766 to 1774, Burke resided at the now vanished Gregories in Beaconsfield from 1768 onwards and, like Waller, is buried at St Mary and All Saints, Beaconsfield.

Just as Wilkes and Burke were contemporaries on the political scene, **William Cowper** and **Thomas Gray** were near contemporaries in the field of literature. Cowper (1731-1800) lived at Olney from 1767 to 1786 and then at Weston Underwood until 1796. He did much of his writing in a stone temple now known as Cowper's Alcove and Grade 2 listed, built in 1753. It has fine views to Olney and Emberton church and there is public access. Gray (1716-71) lived at West End Cottage, Stoke Poges,

Cowper's summerhouse at Weston Underwood.

from 1742 to 1753. He wrote both his famous *Elegy in an English Country Churchyard* and *Ode on a Distant Prospect of Eton College* while at Stoke Poges. The *Elegy* is usually thought to have been inspired by the churchyard of St Giles at Stoke Poges, in which Gray is buried in his mother's tomb, but some make the claim for the churchyard of St Lawrence, Upton-cum-Chalvey (now in Berkshire). Similarly, the *Ode* is also disputed, some maintaining that it was inspired by the view from the terrace of Lord Grenville's home at Dropmore. There is a separate monument to Gray outside the churchyard at Stoke Poges.

For other literary associations, see the entries on Aston Clinton, Beaconsfield, Burnham, Denham, Grendon Underwood, Ivinghoe, Marlow, Newport Pagnell, Weedon, Wendover, Whaddon and Whitchurch. Buckingham is 'Candleford' in Flora Thompson's *Lark Rise to Candleford*, the novelist basing Lark Rise on Juniper Hill in neighbouring Oxfordshire.

11
Folklore, traditions and events

Like other counties, Buckinghamshire has its share of legends and traditions that have survived the passage of centuries.

In **Aylesbury**, 7th October always used to be commemorated as St Osyth Day. Osyth was the Christian daughter of the king of Mercia and was martyred by the Danes in the seventh century AD. She was supposedly born at Quarrendon and buried in St Mary's church at Aylesbury for over forty years before the tomb was moved to Colchester. A holy well at Quarrendon was also linked with Osyth. Similarly, the present names of Well Street and Rumbold Street in **Buckingham** recall St Rumbold. This prodigious infant saint, son of the king of Northumbria, was said to have been born proclaiming himself to be a Christian and demanding baptism. The child preached a sermon but died after only three days. Although he was born in Northamptonshire, St Rumbold's tomb was moved in AD 626 to Buckingham, where the old church, replaced by the present church of St Peter and St Paul in the eighteenth century, had a chapel dedicated to the saint. There was another holy well.

A holy well also figures at **North Marston**, the chalybeate spring there being said to have been brought to light through being struck by the staff of Sir John Schorne. Schorne, who was rector at North Marston from 1290 to 1314, performed other miracles and was credited with conjuring the devil into a boot, hence the Jack-in-the-box. Although he was neither canonised nor beatified, Schorne had a shrine in the church of St Mary at North Marston which became such a focus for pilgrimages that the clerics of Windsor had it removed there in 1481 so that they should benefit from the trade generated. The church at North

Marston still shows traces of the shrine's site in the chancel while 'Sir John Schorne's Well' is also preserved. One further saint connected with the county is St Thomas of Cantelupe (1218-82), Bishop of Hereford and the last English saint before the Reformation, who was born at **Hambleden**.

Boars have a particular significance in two legends. **Boarstall** is supposed to have derived its name from the feat of one Nigel the Huntsman in killing a giant boar terrorising the forest of Bernwood. As a reward, Nigel received the custody of Bernwood from King Edward the Confessor and was given a horn signifying the gift of the manor of Boarstall. A medieval horn is preserved in the County Record Office at Aylesbury together with the Boarstall Cartulary of 1444, which depicts Nigel presenting the boar's head to Edward. In the same way the right to levy the Rhyne Toll at **Chetwode** was granted to the Chetwode family in the twelfth century as a reward for killing another boar in Bernwood. The sound of horns or sea shells being blown would announce the start of a three-day toll levied on all 'foreign' cattle located over 2000 acres (800 hectares) of Bernwood. Some highly questionable relics of the boar were displayed at various times during the nineteenth century but the custom appears to have died out around 1870.

Existing county traditions are of more recent origin. At **Fenny Stratford** each St Martin's Day (11th November) is marked by the firing of the 'Fenny Poppers', six small hand guns, in a local recreation ground. The Poppers, which are kept in St Martin's church, were formerly fired in the churchyard itself to commemorate the building of the church by the eighteenth-century antiquarian Browne

The Ostrich Inn at Colnbrook.

Willis in memory of his parents. Willis's father died on St Martin's Day and his grandfather had lived in St Martin's Lane, London, hence the dedication. At Penn Street a flag is traditionally flown on the mast of an eighteenth-century sailing ship set in the grounds of Penn House to mark the naval victory of Lord Howe at 'The Glorious First of June' in 1794, while at **Hughenden** Disraeli's death in 1881 is marked annually on Primrose Day since primroses were the statesman's favourite flowers. The famous Pancake Race at **Olney** on Shrove Tuesday may well have originated in the fifteenth century as part of the observance of Lent but the present series of annual races was revived only in 1948.

Some rural traditions have survived. On May Day the children of **Nether Winchendon** carry a flower-decorated shrine and garlands from house to house and at **Longwick** children sing to neighbours and parade with traditional May Day crowns and sceptres. Fraw Cup Sunday (the second in the month of May) is traditionally marked at **Ford** and **Haddenham** by picking the last blooms of the snakeshead fritillary. On the first Sunday after 29th June, St Peter's Day is marked at **Wingrave** by the floor of the church of St Peter and St Paul being covered with hay cut from half an acre left to the church.

Some rather unlikely legends have also become associated with Buckinghamshire. Certain features such as Whiteleaf Cross and Bledlow Cross or the glacial erratic left at **Soulbury** during the ice age have acquired a fund of stories over the years. Houses, too, may acquire legends, such as the belief that the ghost of Sir Edmund Verney haunts **Claydon House** in search of the hand cut from his body at the battle of Edgehill in 1642. The seventeenth-century hermit of **Dinton**, John Bigge, was allegedly the executioner of King Charles I, while the original 'Mad Hatter', Roger Crabb, the author of *The English Hermite*, lived at **Chesham**. The Ostrich Inn at **Colnbrook** was reputedly the scene of a series of grisly murders of guests in the seventeenth century. It is perhaps appropriate, therefore, that the proximity to each other of the Cock and Bull inns at **Stony Stratford** is said to have inspired the well-known phrase regarding the veracity of tales.

February
Pancake Race on Shrove Tuesday at Olney. Telephone: 01234 712564.
Milton Keynes Festival of the Arts.

March
High Wycombe Arts Festival. Telephone: 01494 528226.
Aylesbury Arts Festival. Telephone: 01296

86009.

Easter Saturday Races (point-to-point) at Great Kimble.

April

Primrose Day at Hughenden.

Mystery Plays at Long Crendon. Telephone: 01844 208654.

May

May Day ceremony at Nether Winchendon.

May Day Fraw Cup Sunday (second in month) at Haddenham and Ford.

Weighing the Mayor at High Wycombe Guildhall. Telephone: 01494 461000.

Wavendon Festival. Telephone: 01908 582522 or 583928.

June

The Glorious First of June at Penn Street.

St Peter's Day (first Sunday after 29th June) at Wingrave.

Sailing Week at Bourne End.

Marlow Regatta.

Willen Festival.

July

Swan Upping on the river Thames.

September

Bucks County Show (first Thursday).

Amersham Fair.

Wooburn Festival.

High Wycombe Show. Telephone: 01494 421892.

October

Charter Fair at Buckingham.

November

St Martin's Day (11th) firing of Fenny Poppers at St Martin's, Fenny Stratford.

December

Boxing Day meet of hunt in the Market Square, Winslow.

Boxing Day road race in Aylesbury.

12
Tourist information centres

Aylesbury: 8 Bourbon Street, Aylesbury HP20 2RR. Telephone: 01296 330559.

Buckingham: (seasonal) Old Gaol Museum, Market Hill, Buckingham MK18 1EW. Telephone: 01280 823020.

High Wycombe: 6 Cornmarket, High Wycombe HP11 2BW. Telephone: 01494 421892.

Marlow: (seasonal) Court Garden Leisure Centre, Pound Lane, Marlow SL7 2AE. Telephone: 01628 483597.

Milton Keynes: The Food Hall, 411 Secklow Gate East, Central Milton Keynes MK9 3NE. Telephone: 01908 232525 or 231742.

Wendover: Clock Tower, High Street, Wendover HP22 6DU. Telephone: 01296 696759.

Egyptian spring, Hartwell.

13
Further reading

Those especially interested in the past of the county might wish to join the Buckinghamshire Archaeological Society, c/o Bucks County Museum, Church Street, Aylesbury HP20 2QP, which publishes the journal *Records of Bucks*; and the Buckinghamshire Record Society, c/o the Bucks County Record Office, County Hall, Walton Street, Aylesbury HP20 1UA, which publishes an annual volume of historical documents.

Beckett, Ian. *Call to Arms: Buckinghamshire's Citizen Soldiers*. Barracuda, 1985.

Davis, Richard W. *Political Change and Continuity: 1760-1885: A Buckinghamshire Study*. David & Charles, 1972.

Hanley, Hugh. *The Buckinghamshire Sheriffs*. Bucks County Record Office, 1992.

Lawson, Marjorie, and Sparkes, Ivan. *Victorian and Edwardian Buckinghamshire from Old Photographs*. Portman Books, 1976.

Lewis, Shelagh. *Buried Around Buckingham*. Friends of the Old Gaol Museum, 1992.

Reed, Michael. *The Buckinghamshire Landscape*. Hodder & Stoughton, 1979.

Reed, Michael. *A History of Buckinghamshire*. Phillimore, 1993.

Robinson, J. M. *Temples of Delight: Stowe Landscape Garden*s. National Trust and George Philip, 1990.

Watkin, Bruce. *Buckinghamshire*. Faber & Faber, 1981.

Wyatt, Gordon. *Maps of Buckinghamshire*. Barracuda, 1978.

Cottages at Turville.

Index

Page numbers in italic type refer to illustrations.